185 Special Cupcake Recipes

(185 Special Cupcake Recipes - Volume 1)

Angela Haas

Copyright: Published in the United States by Angela Haas/ © ANGELA HAAS

Published on October, 12 2020

All rights reserved. No part of this publication may be reproduced, stored in retrieval system, copied in any form or by any means, electronic, mechanical, photocopying, recording or otherwise transmitted without written permission from the publisher. Please do not participate in or encourage piracy of this material in any way. You must not circulate this book in any format. ANGELA HAAS does not control or direct users' actions and is not responsible for the information or content shared, harm and/or actions of the book readers.

In accordance with the U.S. Copyright Act of 1976, the scanning, uploading and electronic sharing of any part of this book without the permission of the publisher constitute unlawful piracy and theft of the author's intellectual property. If you would like to use material from the book (other than just simply for reviewing the book), prior permission must be obtained by contacting the author at author@bisquerecipes.com

Thank you for your support of the author's rights.

Content

185 AWESOME CUPCAKE RECIPES 6

1. 7 Minute Frosting Recipe 6
2. Apple Crunch Muffins Recipe 6
3. Apple Cupcakes With Cinnamon Marshmallow Frosting Recipe 6
4. April Fools Day "spegetti" Dessert Recipe 7
5. Bacon Maple Cupcakes For Fathers Day Recipe 8
6. Bailey Bites Recipe 8
7. Baklava Ice Cream Bites Recipe 9
8. Baklava Muffins Recipe 10
9. Banana Cupcakes Recipe 10
10. Banana Cupcakes With Ganache Frosting Recipe 11
11. Banana Split Muffins Recipe 11
12. Banana And White Chocolate Cupcakes With Magical Glittering Cream Cheese Frosting Recipe 12
13. Bat Cupcakes 12
14. Best Vanilla Cupcakes Recipe 13
15. Bite Size Cinnamon Cupcakes W/cinnamon Cream Cheese Frosting Recipe 14
16. Black Bottom Cupcakes Recipe 14
17. Black Forest Cheesecake Dessert Cups Recipe 15
18. Black Forrest Muffin Cakes Betty Crocker Recipe 15
19. Black Bottom Apple Cupcakes Recipe 16
20. Blue Monday Banana Muffins Recipe 16
21. Boston Cream Pie Minis Recipe 17
22. Brooklyn Blackout Cupcakes By The Cake Mix Doctor Recipe 17
23. Brownie Cupcakes Recipe 18
24. Brownies Recipe 19
25. Bunny Cupcakes For Kids Of All Ages Recipe 19
26. Bunny Cupcakes Recipe 20
27. Buttermilk Chocolate Cupcakes Recipe 20
28. Buttermilk Iced Pumpkin Cupcakes Recipe 21
29. Cafe Metros Chocolate Cupcakes With Coconut Filling Recipe 22
30. Cappuccino Cupcakes Recipe 22

31. Cappuccino Muffins Recipe 23
32. Caramel Apple Cupcake Recipe 23
33. Carrot Cake W Cream Cheese Frosting Recipe 24
34. Carrot Mini Muffins Recipe 25
35. Carrot Ginger Cupcakes With Spiced Cream Cheese Recipe 25
36. Chai Latte Cupcakes Recipe 26
37. Cheesecake Cookie Cups Recipe 26
38. Chip Lovers Cupcakes Recipe 26
39. Chipper Carrot Cupcakes Recipe 27
40. Choco Raspberry Decadence Recipe 27
41. Chocolate Buttermilk Cupcakes Recipe 28
42. Chocolate Candy Cane Cupcakes Recipe .. 28
43. Chocolate Chiffon Cupcakes Recipe 29
44. Chocolate Chocolate Chip Nut Muffins Recipe 29
45. Chocolate Cream Cheese Cupcakes Recipe 30
46. Chocolate Cupcakes Recipe 30
47. Chocolate Cupcakes Strawberry Chocolate Ganache Vanilla Buttercream Icing Recipe 30
48. Chocolate Cupcakes With Peanut Butter Icing Recipe 31
49. Chocolate Euphoria Muffins Recipe 32
50. Chocolate Mint Chip Cupcakes With Mint Swiss Meringue Buttercream Frosting Recipe 33
51. Chocolate Peanut Butter Cupcakes Recipe 34
52. Chocolate Ricotta Muffins Recipe 34
53. Chocolate Sour Cream Cupcakes Recipe .. 35
54. Chocolate Zucchini And Carrot Cupcakes Recipe 35
55. Chocolate Surprise Muffins Recipe 36
56. Chocolaty Chocolate Chip Muffins Recipe 36
57. Christmas Cupcakes Recipe 36
58. Cincinnati Chili Cupcakes Recipe 37
59. Cinnamon Struesel Cupcakes From The Cupcakery Recipe 38
60. Cinnamon Swirl Snickerdoodle Cupcakes Recipe 38
61. Cinnamon Vanilla Buttercream Frosting Recipe 39
62. Cocoa Velvet Cupcakes Recipe 39
63. Coconut Chocolate Chip Cupcakes Cupcakes Recipe 40

64. Cone A Cake Recipe 41
65. Copycat Starbucks Black Bottom Cupcakes Recipe 41
66. Cotton Candy Cupcakes For Kids Recipe 41
67. Cream Cheese Chocolate Cupcakes Recipe 42
68. Cream Cheese Cupcakes Recipe 42
69. Cream Filled Chocolate Cupcakes Recipe 43
70. Cream Filled Cupcakes Recipe 43
71. Cream Filled Chocolate Cupcakes Recipe 44
72. Creamy Lime Meringue Cupcakes Recipe 45
73. Cupcake Pops Recipe 45
74. Cupcakes Three Ways Vanilla Cupcakes With Chocolate Buttercream And Rasberry Frostings Recipe 46
75. Dark Chocolate Cupcakes With Peanut Butter Filling Recipe 46
76. Devils Food Cake With Brown Sugar Buttercream Recipe 47
77. Devils Food Cupcakes With Marshmallow Filling Recipe 48
78. Diabetic Low Fat Orange Muffins Eggless Recipe 49
79. Double Dark Chocolate Sesame Cakes Recipe 50
80. Double Chocolate Marble Cupcakes Recipe 50
81. Easter Basket Cupcakes Recipe 51
82. Easy Pumpkin Cupcakes Recipe 51
83. Easy Red Velvet Cupcakes Recipe 52
84. Egg Free Chocolate Cupcakes Recipe 52
85. Eileens Cream Cheese Chocolate Cupcakes Recipe 53
86. Elaines Triple Chocolate Muffins Recipe . 53
87. Elvis Cupcakes Recipe 54
88. Espresso Cupcakes With Milk Chocolate Ganache And White Chocolate Frosting Recipe 54
89. Fairy Cakes Recipe 55
90. Favorite Chocolate Cupcakes Recipe 56
91. Frog Cupcakes 56
92. Graveyard Cupcakes Recipe 56
93. Heavenly Cupcakes Recipe 57
94. Hi Hat Cupcakes Recipe 58
95. Hi Hat Cupcakes Recipe 59
96. Ho Ho Cupcakes Recipe 60
97. Honey Cupcakes With Orange Icing Recipe 61
98. Hot Chocolate And Grand Marnier Cupcakes Recipe 61
99. Hot Cocoa Cupcakes Recipe 62
100. Ina Gartens Coconut Cupcakes Recipe 62
101. Irish Car Bomb Cupcakes Recipe 63
102. Key Lime Blossoms Recipe 64
103. Key Lime Cupcakes Recipe 64
104. Lemon Blossoms Little Cupcakes Recipe . 65
105. Lemon Blossoms Recipe 65
106. Lemon Butterfly Cupcakes Recipe 66
107. Lemon Cream Cheese Cupcakes Recipe ... 67
108. Lemon Meringue Cupcakes From The Culinary Institute Of America Recipe 67
109. Lemon Raspberry Cupcakes Recipe 68
110. Light Carrot Cake Cupcakes With Cream Cheese Frosting Recipe 69
111. Little Lemon Yogurt Puffs Recipe 70
112. Little Sacher Cupcakes Recipe 70
113. Magnolia Bakery Red Velvet Cupcakes Recipe 71
114. Mandarin Orange Frosty Recipe 71
115. Margarita Cupcakes Recipe 72
116. Mexi Late Cupcakes Recipe 72
117. Mini OREO Surprise Cupcakes Recipe 73
118. Mini Oreo Cupcakes Recipe 73
119. Mucho Mocha Berry Cupcakes Recipe 74
120. Nana Nog Cupcakes Recipe 74
121. Nigellas Lavendar Cupcakes Recipe 75
122. No Bake Chocolate Cream Cupcakes Recipe 75
123. Nonnas Lemon Ricotta Biscuits Recipe 75
124. Nutella Self Frosting Cupcakes Recipe 76
125. Nutella Or Peanut Butter Cupcakes Recipe 76
126. Oatmeal Raisin Muffins Recipe 77
127. Oreo Cupcakes Recipe 77
128. Paula Deens Crispy Rice Cupcakes Recipe 78
129. Peachy Lemon Muffins Recipe 78
130. Peanut Butter And Jelly Cupcakes Recipe 79
131. Peanut Butter Cup Mousse Cake Recipe ... 79
132. Pecan Streusel Topped Pumpkin Cranberry Muffins Recipe 80
133. Pineapple Coconut And Carrot Cupcakes Recipe 81
134. Pink Peppermint Cupcakes Recipe 82

135. Pink Velvet Cupcakes Recipe 82
136. Pistachio Cupcakes Recipe 83
137. Plum Chocolate Cupcakes With Chocolate Ganache And Walnut Frosting Recipe 83
138. Pretty In Pink Peppermint Cupcakes Recipe 84
139. Pumpkin Cupcakes With Cream Cheese Frosting Recipe 84
140. Pumpkin Cupcakes With Maple Cream Cheese Frosting Recipe 85
141. Pumpkin Ginger Cupcakes 85
142. Rain Drop Cupcakes Recipe 86
143. Red Velvet Cupakes Recipe 86
144. Red Velvet Cupcakes For Two Recipe 87
145. Red Velvet Cupcakes Recipe 87
146. Red Velvet Cupcakes With Cream Cheese Frosting Recipe 88
147. Red Velvet Puffs With Espresso Frosting Recipe 89
148. Rich Double Chocolate Zucchini Muffins Recipe 89
149. Rocky Road Cupcakes Recipe 90
150. Root Beer Cup Cakes Recipe 90
151. Rootbeer Cupcakes With A Butter Cream Glaze Recipe 91
152. Rootbeer Float Cupcakes Recipe 92
153. STRAWBERRY CUPCAKES WITH STRAWBERRY WHIPPED CREAM FROSTING Recipe 93
154. Skinny Hummingbird Cupcakes Recipe 93
155. Snickerdoodle Cupcakes Recipe 94
156. Snowball Cupcakes Recipe 94
157. Spiced Up Cupppycakes With Cream Cheese Frosting Recipe 95
158. Strawberry Cupcakes Recipe 95
159. Strawberry Stuffed Lime Cupcakes Recipe 96
160. Strawberry Tuxedo Cupcakes Recipe 96
161. Strawberry Twinkie Desert Recipe 97
162. Strawberry Cream Cheese Cupcakes Recipe 98
163. Sunshine Cupcakes 98
164. Surprise Cupcake Recipe 98
165. Sweet Hearts Recipe 99
166. The Magnolia Bakery Cupcake Recipe Recipe 99
167. The Easiest Chocolate Muffins In The World Recipe 99
168. Tie Die Cupcakes Or Cake Recipe 100
169. Tiramisu Cupcakes Recipe 100
170. Toll House Cupcakes Recipe.................... 101
171. Topping 2 For Muffins And Scones Recipe 101
172. Tripple Chocolate Muffins Recipe 101
173. Ultimate Chocolate Cupcakes With Ganache Filling Recipe 102
174. Valentine Fairy Cakes Recipe 103
175. Valentines Day Red Velvet Cup Cakes Recipe 104
176. Vanilla Bean Coconut Cupcakes With Coconut Frosting Recipe 105
177. Vanilla Cupcake With Fruit Topping Recipe 106
178. Warm Chocolate Cupcake With Decadent Soft Chocolate Center Recipe 106
179. White Chocolate Macadamia Nut Cupcakes Recipe 107
180. White Chocolate Mousse In Milk Chocolate Shells Recipe 107
181. White Russian Cupcakes Recipe 108
182. Whole Wheat Cupcakes Recipe 109
183. Wigglin Jigglin Halloween Cupcakes Recipe 109
184. White Chocolate Macadamia Cupcakes Recipe 110
185. Yellow Cake Cupcakes Recipe 110

INDEX **111**

CONCLUSION **113**

185 Awesome Cupcake Recipes

***

1. 7 Minute Frosting Recipe

Serving: 36 | Prep: | Cook: 12mins | Ready in:

Ingredients

- 1 1/2 cups sugar
- 1/4 teaspoon cream of tartar or 1 tablespoon white corn syrup
- 1/8 teaspoon salt
- 1/3 cup water
- 2 egg whites
- 1 1/2 teaspoons pure vanilla extract

Direction

- Place sugar, cream of tartar or corn syrup, salt, water, and egg whites in the top of a double boiler.
- Beat with a handheld electric mixer for 1 minute.
- Place pan over boiling water, being sure that boiling water does not touch the bottom of the top pan. (If this happens, it could cause your frosting to become grainy).
- Beat constantly on high speed with electric mixer for 7 minutes.
- Beat in vanilla.

2. Apple Crunch Muffins Recipe

Serving: 12 | Prep: | Cook: 25mins | Ready in:

Ingredients

- apple Crunch Muffins
- 1-1/2 c. flour
- 1/2 c. sugar
- 1 T. baking powder
- 1 t. cinnamon
- 1/2 t. salt
- 1 egg
- 1/2 c. dry milk
- 1/4 c. oil
- 1 c. coarsely shredded unpeeled apple 1/3 c. packed brown sugar
- 1/2 c. chopped walnuts

Direction

- Instructions
- Mix flour, sugar (granulated) with 1/2 t. cinnamon and salt. Stir in egg, milk, oil, and apple until just moistened. Bake at 400 degrees for 25 minutes or test with pick. Makes 12 muffins per recipe.

3. Apple Cupcakes With Cinnamon Marshmallow Frosting Recipe

Serving: 12 | Prep: | Cook: 20mins | Ready in:

Ingredients

- Makes: 12 cupcakes
- Total Time: 2 hr 30 min
- Cook Time: 20 min
- Ingredients:
- Cupcakes
- 1-1/2 cups shredded peeled apples
- 1/2 cup diced dried apples
- 3 tablespoons packed light brown sugar
- 3/4 cup packed light brown sugar
- 1 teaspoon ground cinnamon, divided
- 1/3 cup canola oil
- 2 large eggs

- 1 teaspoon vanilla extract
- 3/4 cup whole-wheat pastry flour
- 3/4 cup cake flour
- 3/4 teaspoon baking soda
- 1/4 teaspoon salt
- 1/2 cup low-fat buttermilk
- NOTE: Any frosting/icing will do.
- frosting
- 1 cup light brown sugar
- 1/4 cup water
- 4 teaspoons (equivalent to 2 egg whites) dried egg whites (see Tips), reconstituted according to package directions
- 1/4 teaspoon cream of tartar
- Pinch of salt
- 1 teaspoon vanilla extract
- 1/2 teaspoon ground cinnamon, plus more for garnish

Direction

- To prepare cupcakes:
- Preheat oven to 350°F. Line 12 (1/2-cup) muffin cups with cupcake liners or coat with cooking spray.
- Combine shredded and dried apples in a bowl with 3 tablespoons brown sugar and 1/4 teaspoon cinnamon. Set aside. Beat oil and the remaining 3/4 cup brown sugar in a large mixing bowl with an electric mixer on medium speed until well combined. Beat in eggs one at a time until combined. Add vanilla, increase speed to high, and beat for 1 minute.
- Whisk whole-wheat flour, cake flour, baking soda, salt, and the remaining 3/4 teaspoon cinnamon in a medium bowl.
- With the mixer on low speed, alternately add the dry ingredients and buttermilk to the batter, starting and ending with dry ingredients and scraping the sides of the bowl as needed, until just combined. Stir in the reserved apple mixture until just combined. Divide the batter among the prepared muffin cups. (The cups will be full.)
- Bake the cupcakes until a toothpick inserted into the centre of a cake comes out clean, 20 to 22 minutes. Let cool on a wire rack for at least 1 hour before frosting.
- To prepare frosting:
- Bring 2 inches of water to a simmer in the bottom of a double boiler. Combine 1 cup brown sugar and 1/4 cup water in the top of the double boiler. Heat over the simmering water, stirring, until the sugar has dissolved, 2 to 3 minutes. Add reconstituted egg whites, cream of tartar, and pinch of salt. Beat with an electric mixer on high speed until the mixture is glossy and thick, 5 to 7 minutes. Remove the top pan from the heat and continue beating for 1 minute more to cool. Add vanilla and 1/2 teaspoon cinnamon and beat on low just to combine. Spread or pipe the frosting onto the cooled cupcakes and sprinkle cinnamon on top, if desired.
- Tips
- Ingredient note: Dried egg whites are pasteurized, so this product is a wise choice in dishes that call for an uncooked meringue. Look for brands like Just Whites in the baking or natural-foods section of most supermarkets or online at bakerscatalogue.com.
- Carb Servings: 1 starch, 2 other carbohydrates, 1 fat. Carbohydrate Servings: 3.

4. April Fools Day "spegetti" Dessert Recipe

Serving: 7 | Prep: | Cook: 15mins | Ready in:

Ingredients

- 7 white cupcakes (Homemade or store bought with white frosting)
- 1 jar strawberry jam
- 1 block white chocolate
- thick white frosting for piping
- 7 chocolate truffles

Direction

- On a large serving plate place one cupcake in the centre and surround tightly with the test of the cupcakes to make a circle.
- Fill frosting tube with white frosting and attach a circle hole nozzle about the size of spaghetti.
- Pipe over the cupcakes, hap hazard until it looks like a plate of spaghetti.
- Top with some strawberry jam to look like sauce.
- Put truffles (Meatballs) on top.
- Grate white chocolate over top to resemble parmesan cheese.

5. Bacon Maple Cupcakes For Fathers Day Recipe

Serving: 24 | Prep: | Cook: 1hours | Ready in:

Ingredients

- butter cake:
- 1 1/2 cups flour
- 1 tsp salt
- 2 tsp baking powder
- 1 cup sugar
- 2 eggs
- 1 tsp vanila
- 3/4 cup milk
- Cream ceese frosting:
- 1 8oz pack cheese
- 1 stick of butter
- 2 cups powder sugar
- 2 tsp maple syrup
- pinch of salt
- splash of half and half or cream
- candied bacon:
- cook 6 strips of thick cut bacon til nearly done then sprinkle generously with brown sugar and continue to cook, flipping bacon often, till candied and crisp.

Direction

- Cream butter sugar butter and salt till fluffy
- Add eggs and stir
- Add sifted flour and baking soda and milk alternately
- Pour into greased and floured cupcake pan, I used mini cupcake pan
- Bake at 350* till fluffy and slightly brown, cool
- Make candied bacon set aside to cool
- Make frosting once cakes are cooled and frost generously
- To make frosting cream room temp butter and cream cheese together
- Add vanilla and sugar and stir, add cream if to dry
- TOP IT OFF WITH SHARDS OF BROKEN UP CANDIED BACON!
- No man can resist!

6. Bailey Bites Recipe

Serving: 50 | Prep: | Cook: 120mins | Ready in:

Ingredients

- 2 cups cake flour
- 2 teaspoons baking powder
- 1/2 teaspoon salt
- 2 cups sugar
- 1/2 cup butter
- 1 teaspoon vanilla
- 1/2 cup milk
- 2 eggs
- 4 ounces unsweetened chocolate, melted
- 1 cup Bailey's irish cream
- 1 cup chopped walnuts

Direction

- Preheat oven to 350 degrees.
- Sift first 3 ingredients together; set aside.
- Cream sugar and butter until light and fluffy; add eggs one at a time, beat well after each addition.
- Mix in chocolate and vanilla.

- Mix Bailey's with milk and add alternately with flour, mixing well.
- Add nuts.
- Spoon into mini cupcake liners and bake for about 9-12 minutes.
- Makes a bunch!
- I honestly don't know how long the overall cook time is because I always make these all day long with the other Irish goodies.

7. Baklava Ice Cream Bites Recipe

Serving: 16 | Prep: | Cook: 20mins | Ready in:

Ingredients

- I tried to include freezer time in the prep time!
- ~
- vanilla ice cream - get the best quality possible
- 16 sheets of phyllo
- 2 small packages of chopped walnuts or pistachios, your choice
- honey
- 1/2 stick of butter, room temp

Direction

- Put a cookie tray in the freezer for 10 minutes.
- Take out of freezer and line with parchment paper.
- Scoop approx. 16 balls of vanilla ice cream with a mini scoop.
- Place on parchment paper and return cookie sheet to the freezer for 1 hour or until frozen solid.
- Preheat oven to 350 F.
- Melt butter in microwave or in a pan.
- Remove phyllo dough from fridge.
- Place sheets in between 2 wet paper towels.
- Place one sheet of phyllo on a clean surface.
- With a pastry brush, brush dough well with melted butter.
- Continue in this fashion until you have 4 sheets on top of each other.
- With a pizza cutter, cut the dough into 8 squares which are still 4 layers thick.
- Repeat 3 times until you have 16 squares.
- Places squares into mini muffin tin and mould into cups, bake in the oven for 20-30 minutes or until dough is golden brown.
- Remove from oven and set aside.
- After one hour is up, place walnuts in a shallow baking dish or pie pan.
- Remove ice cream balls from the freezer and roll them in the nuts.
- Place back on cookie sheet and place in freezer for another 1/2 hour.
- After the 1/2 hour remove ice cream coated balls from the freezer, place each one into a phyllo cup and drizzle with honey.
- Serve immediately!
- ==
- This dessert is the final instalment to my Mediterranean Medley class I taught last week at
- The Culinary which is inside Bakers & Cooks here in Ocala, FL.
- I developed this recipe to try to emulate the flavours of baklava without all the work involved and without all the sweetness. I know, I know, I love Baklava like the rest of you and I know that the sweetness is what really makes it, but I was looking for a way to introduce people who may not have had baklava to the flavours, or give those who enjoy baklava another take on it. Plus, who doesn't love ice cream?! Those little banana bites I did a while back were so cute I just wanted to keep the theme of bite sized goodies that are so flavourful and delicious you only need a bite to feel satisfied! These are the perfect little dessert for a BBQ, movie or game night or anytime you feel a craving for a little something sweet!
- Also, here is a little reminder - if you would like to participate in the FIRST monthly Leftover Queen Foodie Event - The Royal Foodie Joust, you have until midnight TONIGHT (EST US) to enter. Click here for more details!

8. Baklava Muffins Recipe

Serving: 12 | Prep: | Cook: 15mins | Ready in:

Ingredients

- Filling:
- scant 1/2 cup (50g) chopped walnuts (I have pecans and almonds, so that is what I am going to use.)
- 1/3 cup (67g) sugar
- 1 1/2 teaspoons ground cinnamon
- 3 tablespoons (42g) unsalted butter, melted
- ~
- Muffins:
- 1 cup + 7 tablespoons (210g) all purpose flour
- 2 teaspoons baking powder
- 1/2 teaspoon baking soda
- 1/4 cup (50g) sugar
- 1 large egg
- 3 tablespoons (42g) unsalted butter, melted
- 1 cup + 2 tablespoons buttermilk
- ~
- Topping:
- about 1/2 cup honey

Direction

- Preheat the oven to 200°C/400°F.
- Line a 12-cup muffin pan with paper baking cups.
- Mix all the filling ingredients in a small bowl, set aside.
- In a large bowl, sift together the flour, baking powder and baking soda; add sugar.
- In a wide-mouthed measuring cup, whisk the egg, melted butter and buttermilk.
- Make a well in the dry ingredients and pour in the liquid.
- Mix lightly and gently, remembering to keep it bumpy – I used a fork to mix it.
- Fill the cups 1/3 full, add a scant tablespoon of filling, and then cover with more muffin batter until 2/3 full.
- Bake for 15 minutes, or until golden brown.
- Remove the muffins from the pan and place them on a rack. Drizzle with honey.
- Makes 12 – each well in my muffin pan holds 1/3 cup batter and I got 11 muffins

9. Banana Cupcakes Recipe

Serving: 18 | Prep: | Cook: 20mins | Ready in:

Ingredients

- ¼ cup butter
- ¼ cup solid Crisco
- 1 cup sugar
- 1 teaspoon vanilla extract
- 2 eggs
- 2 cups plus 2 tablespoons flour
- 2½ teaspoons baking powder
- ½ teaspoon salt
- ¼ teaspoon baking soda
- 1 cup mashed bananas (about 3 medium bananas)
- ¼ cup buttermilk or sour cream (I always use sour cream)

Direction

- In a large bowl, cream together the butter, Crisco, sugar and extract.
- Beat in eggs, one at a time.
- Mix dry ingredients together and add to creamed mixture alternately with bananas and sour cream (or buttermilk).
- Grease 18 muffin tins (or line tins with cupcake liners); fill tins 3/4 full (I always get exactly 18 out of this recipe).
- Bake at 375 degrees for 20 minutes.
- Cool and frost. One frosting option is listed below
- Brown Sugar Frosting:
- 6 tablespoons brown sugar
- 4 tablespoons whole milk or half and half
- 4 tablespoons butter
- Powdered sugar

- ½ teaspoon vanilla extract
- Combine brown sugar, milk and butter in saucepan; bring to a boil. Remove pan from heat; beat in enough powdered sugar to make frosting spreadable; beat in vanilla.

10. Banana Cupcakes With Ganache Frosting Recipe

Serving: 20 | Prep: | Cook: 20mins | Ready in:

Ingredients

- 2 cups all-purpose flour
- 1-1/2 cups Pure Cane sugar
- 3/4 teaspoon baking soda
- 1/2 teaspoon baking powder
- 1/2 teaspoon salt
- 2 eggs
- 1/2 cup canola oil
- 1/4 cup buttermilk
- 1 teaspoon vanilla extract
- 1-1/3 cups mashed ripe bananas (2 to 3 medium)
- 3/4 cup chopped pecans
- FROSTING:
- 7 squares (1 ounce each) semisweet chocolate, chopped
- 1/2 cup heavy whipping cream
- 6 tablespoons shortening
- 1/3 cup powdered sugar
- 1/2 cup marshmallow creme
- 1/2 teaspoon vanilla extract

Direction

- In a large bowl, combine the flour, sugar, baking soda, baking powder and salt.
- In another bowl, combine the eggs, oil, buttermilk and vanilla.
- Beat into dry ingredients just until moistened.
- Fold in bananas and pecans.
- Fill paper-lined muffin cups two-thirds full.
- Bake at 350° for 20-24 minutes or until a toothpick comes out clean.
- Cool for 5 minutes before removing from pans to wire racks to cool completely.
- For frosting, in a small saucepan, melt chocolate with cream over low heat; stir until blended.
- Remove from the heat.
- Transfer to a small bowl; cool until mixture reaches room temperature.
- In a large bowl, cream shortening and confectioners' sugar until light and fluffy.
- Beat in marshmallow crème and vanilla.
- Add chocolate mixture.
- Beat until light and fluffy.
- Frost cupcakes.
- Yield: about 1-1/2 dozen.

11. Banana Split Muffins Recipe

Serving: 18 | Prep: | Cook: 35mins | Ready in:

Ingredients

- 1/2 cup butter or butter substitute
- 1 cup brown sugar
- 1 egg
- 3 ripe bananas' mashed
- 1 cup chocolate chips
- 1/2 cup chopped walnuts
- 1 1/2 cup flour
- 1 tsp baking powder
- 1 tsp baking soda

Direction

- Cream butter and sugar add egg. Combine with mashed bananas, flour, baking soda and baking powder.
- Add chocolate chips and nuts. Place muffins cups into muffin pan or light butter pan if you prefer not to use cups. Divide evenly into 18 and bake at 325 degrees for 35 minutes.
- Top with a pineapple frosting - 2 cups of confectioners' sugar, 2 tbsps. butter (softened),

1/4 cup well drained pineapple (blot to remove all juices) 2- 3 tbsps. of cream to make the frosting smooth.
- Spread with frosting and add a cherry.....enjoy.

12. Banana And White Chocolate Cupcakes With Magical Glittering Cream Cheese Frosting Recipe

Serving: 12 | Prep: | Cook: 22mins | Ready in:

Ingredients

- banana and white chocolate Cupcakes
- 150g unsalted butter, at room temperature
- 150g caster sugar
- 1 very ripe banana, peeled and mashed
- 2 large free range eggs
- 125g plain flour
- 25g cornflour
- 1tsp baking powder
- 50g white chocolate chips
- Preheat the oven to 180°C and line a large muffin tray with 12 cupcake cases.
- Cream the soft butter and sugar until pale and fluffy.
- Add the mashed banana, cream until well incorporated, add the eggs one at a time, cream well after each addition.
- Sift the flour, baking powder and cornflour over the creamed banana mixture and add the white chocolate chips, fold it all together. Do not over work the cupcake batter.
- Fill a disposable piping bag with the cupcake batter and fill each case three quarters full.
- Bake the cupcakes in the preheated oven for 20 - 22 minutes, test if they are baked by inserting a metal skewer if the skewer comes out clean then the cupcakes are done.
- Transfer the cupcakes to a cooling rack and let them cool completely before decorating them with the cream cheese frosting.

Direction

- Alejandro's Cream Cheese Frosting
- 100g cream cheese, (Philadelphia is perfect for this)
- 200g icing sugar, sifted
- 25g unsalted butter, melted and cooled
- Whip the sifted icing sugar and cream cheese until light and fluffy. I use a mixer with a whisk attachment for this stage.
- Pour the cooled melted butter slowly into the whipping cream cheese mixture, whip the cream cheese mixture for a couple of minutes to incorporate air.
- Let the cream cheese frosting set in the fridge for at least one hour before using. This frosting is best made the day before required so that it can set slightly and get a fantastic gloss.
- This frosting is fairly soft, take it out of the fridge for 20 minute before needed to come to room temperature.
- Garnish the cupcakes with the cream cheese frosting and make it look extra pretty with silver balls and edible glitter.
- Makes 12 cupcakes
- I buy the edible glitter from our local cake craft shop. Please make sure that the glitter is edible, do not use craft glitter. I also found this website that sells it for a very reasonable price, Celebration Toppers. A small tub goes a very long way providing you apply the glitter with a small brush. I found a very fine brush at the same cake shop however you could alternatively buy a cheap painters brush from a craft shop. Dip the dry brush into the glitter and shake it over the iced cupcakes to apply a bit of glitz and sparkle to your cupcakes.

13. Bat Cupcakes

Serving: 0 | Prep: | Cook: |Ready in:

Ingredients

- 1 package chocolate cake mix (regular size)

- 1 can (16 ounces) chocolate frosting
- 24 fudge-striped cookies
- 24 milk chocolate kisses
- White decorating icing

Direction

- Prepare and bake cake mix according to package directions for cupcakes. Cool completely.
- Spread frosting over cupcakes. For bat wings, cut cookies in half; insert two cookie halves into each cupcake.
- Gently press chocolate kisses into frosting for heads. Add eyes with decorating icing.
- Nutrition Facts
- 1 cupcake: 284 calories, 14g fat (5g saturated fat), 27mg cholesterol, 249mg sodium, 37g carbohydrate (25g sugars, 1g fiber), 3g protein.

14. Best Vanilla Cupcakes Recipe

Serving: 12 | Prep: | Cook: 15mins | Ready in:

Ingredients

- 1 cup of softened butter
- 2 cups of granulated sugar
- 3 cups of sifted cake flour
- 3 tsp. baking powder
- 1/2 tsp. salt
- 4 eggs
- 1 cup of whipping cream
- 2 tsp. vanilla extract
- 1/2 tsp. almond extract
- *You will end up with enough extra batter. I make a loaf cake out of the excess which comes out like a butter pound cake. I cook the loaf, cool it and wrap it in saran wrap and freeze for later.

Direction

- Preheat the oven to 350 degrees.
- Place cupcake inserts into a muffin pan.
- Sift the flour with the baking powder and salt.
- Cream your butter in a separate mixing bowl and add sugar.
- Blend sugar and butter together for at least 3 minutes, scraping down the sides.
- Add one egg at a time, beating well after each addition.
- Once the batter is well-blended, add one cup of flour and blend and then add a half a cup of the cream and blend.
- Repeat flour then cream.
- Add the extracts and blend quickly until smooth.
- Spoon the batter into the cupcake cups, filling to 1/2 full.
- Save the leftover batter!
- Place in oven and bake for 15-20 minutes until firm.
- Remove from oven and cool in the pan.
- Frosting:
- 4 cups of powdered sugar
- 1 stick of butter
- 2 tsp. pure vanilla extract
- 3 tsp. of water or milk or cream
- Blend all together and spread over cupcakes.
- I cut a hole in a Ziploc baggie and insert a frosting tip. Tilting the bag with your hand, fill up the bottom of the bag with the frosting and twist the top tightly so that the frosting moves towards the tip. I used a star tip and just made a swirl or "snail" type of design and sprinkled just a few round candies on top for colour.
- If you use water instead of milk or cream, your frosting will dry nicely and give each bite a nice little crunch. I let my cupcakes dry overnight. I just cover them with cellophane.
- If you use cream, your frosting will be softer in texture. Using milk is a standard ingredient for a basic buttercream frosting. I don't think that it matters at all to the children who get to eat the cupcakes.

15. Bite Size Cinnamon Cupcakes W/cinnamon Cream Cheese Frosting Recipe

Serving: 0 | Prep: | Cook: 30mins | Ready in:

Ingredients

- For the Cupcakes
- 3/4 C whole wheat pastry flour
- 3/4 C all-purpose flour
- 1 1/2 tsp baking powder
- 1/4 tsp salt
- 2 tsp cinnamon
- 1/2 tsp nutmeg
- 2/3 C granulated sugar substitute
- 1/4 C butter, softened
- 1/4 C non-fat plain yogurt
- 2 Land O' Lakes All-Natural Farm Fresh eggs
- 1/2 C non-fat milk
- 1 1/2 tsp vanilla extract
- For the frosting
- 1 C powdered sugar
- 2 tbsp butter, softened
- 4 oz. 1/3 fat neufchatel cheese
- 2 tsp cinnamon
- 1/4 tsp nutmeg
- 1 tsp vanilla
- 2-3 tsp non-fat milk

Direction

- 1. Preheat oven to 350. Place mini cupcake liners in mini muffin tin.
- 2. Combine whole wheat pastry flour, all-purpose flour, baking powder, salt, cinnamon, and nutmeg in a medium-sized bowl. Set aside.
- 3. In the bowl of a stand mixer, add sugar substitute and butter. Beat until creamy. Add in the yogurt and eggs. Scrape sides of bowl and beat until well-mixed. Stir in milk and vanilla alternately with the flour mixture until just combined.
- 4. Spoon cupcake batter into liners. Fill cups about 2/3 full. Bake for 8-10 minutes or until centre is set. Cool for 10 minutes in pan and then remove to wire rack to cool completely.
- 5. While cupcakes are cooling, prepare frosting. Combine powdered sugar, butter, Neufchatel cheese, cinnamon, nutmeg, and vanilla in a mixing bowl. Beat until smooth. Slowly add in the milk, a teaspoon at a time, to reach desired consistency.
- 6. Lightly swirl frosting on cupcakes. Enjoy!
- 7. Store leftover cupcakes in refrigerator.

16. Black Bottom Cupcakes Recipe

Serving: 24 | Prep: | Cook: 25mins | Ready in:

Ingredients

- For filling: 16 ounces cream cheese, at room temperature
- 1/2 cup sugar
- 1/4 teaspoon salt
- 2 large egg whites, at room temperature
- 2 tablespoons sour cream, at room temperature
- 1/3 cup miniature chocolate chips (about 2 oz) (*Do not substitute regular chocolate chips for the miniature chips. Regular chips are much heavier and will sink to the bottom of the cupcakes. I used nestle semi-sweet miniatures and they worked well)
- For cupcakes: 1 1/2 cups all-purpose flour
- 1/2 cup Dutch-processed cocoa powder
- 1 1/4 cups sugar
- 1/2 tsp salt
- 1 1/4 tsp baking soda
- 3/4 cup sour cream, at room temperature
- 1 1/3 cups water
- 1/2 cup (1 stick) unsalted butter, melted and slightly cooled
- 1 tsp vanilla extract

Direction

- Adjust oven rack to lower-middle position and heat oven to 350 degrees. Line 2 standard muffin tins with cupcake liners.
- For filling: With electric mixer on medium speed, beat cream cheese, sugar, and salt in medium bowl until smooth, about 30 seconds. Beat in egg whites and sour cream until combined, about 1 minute. Stir in chocolate chips and set aside.
- For cupcakes: Whisk sugar, salt, flour, cocoa, and baking soda in a large bowl. Make a well in the centre and add the sour cream, water, butter, and vanilla; whisk until just combined.
- Divide batter evenly among 24 cupcake liners and top each with 1 rounded tablespoon of the cream cheese mixture.
- Bake for about 20-25 minutes, until tops of cupcakes just begin to crack or until a toothpick inserted into the "cake" part of the cupcake comes out with a few moist crumbs on it. I recommend that you start checking on the cupcakes after 20 minutes because you don't want them to dry out.
- Cool cupcakes in tins for 10 minutes before transferring to wire rack to cool completely. (Cupcakes can be refrigerated in airtight container for up to 2 days.)

17. Black Forest Cheesecake Dessert Cups Recipe

Serving: 24 | Prep: | Cook: 250mins | Ready in:

Ingredients

- 1 box (19.5 oz) pillsbury Brownie classics traditional fudge brownie mix
- 1/2 cup vegetable oil
- 1/4 cup water
- 4 eggs
- 1 cup semisweet chocolate chips (6oz)
- 2 packages (8 oz each) cream cheese, softened
- 1/2 cup granulated sugar
- 1 container (6 oz0 yoplait Thick & Creamy vanilla yogurt
- 1 can 921 oz0 cherry pie filling
- 1 aerosol can whipped cream topping

Direction

- Heat oven to 350*Place paper baking cup in each of 24 large muffin cups (2 3/4 inches in diameter and 1 1/4 inches deep). Make brownie mix as directed on box using oil, water and 2 of the eggs. Divide batter evenly among muffin cups (about 2 tablespoon per cup). Bake 15 minutes.
- Meanwhile, in small microwavable bowl, microwave chocolate chips on high 1 minute. Stir and microwave in 15-second increments, stirring after each, until chips are melted and smooth; set aside. In large bowl, beat cream cheese with electric mixer on medium speed until smooth. Beat in sugar, remaining 2 eggs and yogurt until blended. Add melted chocolate; beat until well blended.
- Divide chocolate mixture evenly over warm brownie layer in cups (about 3 tablespoons per cup, filling each to top of cup. Cups will be full.
- Bake 22-26 minutes longer or until set. Cool in pans 20 to 30 minutes. Carefully remove dessert cups from pan (cream cheese mixture will be soft); place on serving platter. Refrigerate at least 1 hour before serving.
- To serve, remove paper; top each dessert cup with 1 tablespoon pie filling (including 2 or 3 cherries) and 1 tablespoon whipped cream topping. If desired, arrange cupcakes on pedestal cake plate covered with linen napkin....Store in refrigerator

18. Black Forrest Muffin Cakes Betty Crocker Recipe

Serving: 12 | Prep: | Cook: 30mins | Ready in:

Ingredients

- 1 box (1 lb 2.25 oz) Betty Crocker® double chocolate muffin mix
- 1 can (21 oz) cherry pie filling
- 1 egg
- Frozen (thawed) whipped topping, if desired
- 12 maraschino cherries, if desired

Direction

- 1. Heat oven to 400°F. Place paper baking cup in each of 12 regular-size muffin cups.
- 2. In medium bowl, stir muffin mix, pie filling and egg until blended (batter will be very moist). Divide batter among muffin cups.
- 3. Bake 28 to 30 minutes or until tops spring back when touched. Cool 5 minutes; carefully remove from pan to cooling rack. Cool completely, about 30 minutes. Serve each cake topped with dollop of whipped topping and a cherry.
- High Altitude (3500-6500 ft.): Place paper baking cup in each of 18 regular-size muffin cups. Stir 2 tablespoons Gold Medal® all-purpose flour into dry muffin mix.

19. Black Bottom Apple Cupcakes Recipe

Serving: 12 | Prep: | Cook: 30mins | Ready in:

Ingredients

- 1 1/2 lb granny smith apples, peeled, halved, cored and cut in 1/2-inch pieces (4 cups)
- 3/4 cup packed light-brown sugar
- 1 T unsalted stick butter
- 6 oz cream cheese, softened
- 1 large egg
- 3/4 cup all purpose flour
- 1/2 cup apple juice
- 3 T each oil and unsweetened cocoa powder
- 1 1/2 tsp cider vinegar
- 1 tsp vanilla extract
- 1/2 tsp each baking soda and cinamon
- 1/4 tsp salt

Direction

- Heat oven to 350. Line 12 regular-size (2 1/2-inch-diameter) muffin cups with paper liners.
- Heat a large non-stick skillet over high heat. Stir in apples, 1/4 cup brown sugar and the butter. Cook, stirring once, 5 minutes or until apples are caramelized. Let cool.
- Meanwhile beat cream cheese, 1/4 cup brown sugar and the egg in a small bowl with mixer on medium speed 1 minute or until smooth, light and fluffy. Set aside.
- Put remaining 1/4 cup brown sugar and rest of ingredients (except cooked apples) in a medium bowl; stir with a wire whisk until well blended. Divide evenly among muffin cups. Top each with 1 T apples, 1 heaping T cream cheese mixture, and then the remaining apples.
- Bake 30 minutes or until cheese mixture has puffed and set. Cool in pan on a wire rack 5 minutes before removing from pan to rack to cool completely. Remove paper liners before serving.
- Per cupcake: 211 calories; 10 g fat; 29 g carb

20. Blue Monday Banana Muffins Recipe

Serving: 21 | Prep: | Cook: 25mins | Ready in:

Ingredients

- 3 large, ripe bananas, mashed
- 1/4 cup non-fat plain yogurt
- 1 tsp lemon juice
- 1 tbsp vanilla extract
- 1/2 tsp banana extract
- 2 tsp blue food colouring (optional)
- 2 cups flour
- 1 tsp baking powder
- 3/4 tsp baking soda
- 1/2 tsp salt
- 1/2 cup softened butter

- 1 1/2 cups sugar
- 6 oz silken tofu, pureed

Direction

- Preheat oven to 350F, grease or line muffin cups with paper liners.
- In a medium bowl, combine bananas, yogurt, lemon juice, extracts and food colouring. Set aside.
- In another medium bowl, whisk together the flour, baking powder, baking soda and salt. Set aside.
- In a large bowl, cream butter and sugar until fluffy.
- Add tofu, beating well to combine.
- Beginning and ending with the dry mixture, alternate additions of flour and banana mixtures, beating well after each addition.
- Bake for 20-25 minutes, until they test done.
- Turn out immediately and cool completely on a wire rack.

21. Boston Cream Pie Minis Recipe

Serving: 24 | Prep: | Cook: 45mins | Ready in:

Ingredients

- 1 pkg (2 layer size) yellow cake mix
- 1 pkg (3.4oz) vanilla instant pudding
- 1 c cold milk
- 1-1/2 c thawed whipped topping, divided
- 4 squares semi-sweet chocolate

Direction

- Heat oven to 350.
- Prepare cake batter and bake as directed on pkg. for 24 cupcakes. Cool completely.
- Beat pudding mix and milk with whisk 2 mins. Let stand 5 mins. Meanwhile, use serrated knife to cut cupcakes in half horizontally. Stir 1/2 c whipped topping into pudding. Spoon into bottom halves of cupcakes, using about 1 Tbsp. for each. Cover with cupcake tops.
- Microwave remaining whipped topping and chocolate in microwaveable bowl on high 1-1/2 mins, or till chocolate is almost melted, stirring after 1 min. Stir till chocolate is completely melted and mixture is well blended. Let stand 15 mins. Spread onto cupcakes. Refrigerate 15 mins before serving.

22. Brooklyn Blackout Cupcakes By The Cake Mix Doctor Recipe

Serving: 20 | Prep: | Cook: 27mins | Ready in:

Ingredients

- Brooklyn Blackout Cupcakes by the cake mix Doctor
- ---
- Brooklyn Blackout Cupcakes
- Filling and frosting
- 1 (3 1/2 ounce) package cook and serve chocolate pudding mix
- 2 cups whole milk
- 1/2 cup semi-sweet chocolate chips
- 2 tablespoons butter
- 1 teaspoon vanilla extract
- cakes
- 1 (18 1/4 ounce) box plain devil's food cake mix
- 3 tablespoons Dutch-processed cocoa powder
- 1 1/2 cups buttermilk
- 1/2 cup canola oil
- 3 large eggs
- 1 teaspoon vanilla extract
- .

Direction

- Make the filling and frosting: place the pudding mix and milk in a 2-qt saucepan over medium-high heat. Whisk constantly until the mixture comes to a boil and thickens, 4-5 minutes. Turn off the heat.

- Add the chocolate chips, butter, and vanilla and stir until the chips and butter melts, 2 minutes.
- Remove the pan from the heat and cover the pudding with plastic wrap placed directly on its surface. Let cool for 45 minutes at room temperature.
- Meanwhile, preheat the oven to 350°F Line 24 cupcake wells with paper liners.
- Make the batter: place the cake mix, cocoa powder, buttermilk, oil, eggs, and vanilla in a large mixing bowl. Blend with an electric mixer on low speed for 30 seconds. Stop the mixer and scrape down the sides of the bowl.
- Increase the mixer speed to medium and beat 2 minutes more. Batter will be thick. Scoop 1/4 cup batter into each cupcake well you should get 24.
- Bake for 17-20 minutes, until tops are springy when lightly pressed. Cool in the pans on wire racks for 5 minutes.
- Remove 4 cupcakes from the pans and crumble them into a bowl, making coarse crumbs. Loosen the remaining cupcakes from the pans and cool them on wire racks for 15 minutes.
- Divide the pudding mixture into 2 portions. Fit a pastry bag with a large round tip and spoon 1 cup of the filling into the bag. Gently push the tip into the centre of each cupcake and squirt a generous amount of pudding inside. Refill the bag as needed and repeat for all 20 cakes.
- Place a heaping tablespoons of the remaining pudding portion on the top of each cupcake and spread to cover the entire surface. Top the frosting with a sprinkling of cupcake crumbs, pressing down slightly so they stick.
- Store uneaten cupcakes covered in the refrigerator for up to 5 days.
- Yield 20 servings
- From the Cake Mix Doctor

23. Brownie Cupcakes Recipe

Serving: 12 | Prep: | Cook: 20mins | Ready in:

Ingredients

- Brownie Cupcakes:
- 4 ounces (120 grams) unsweetened chocolate, chopped
- 1/2 cup (113 grams) unsalted butter, cut into pieces
- 1 1/4 cup (250 grams) granulated white sugar
- 1 teaspoon pure vanilla extract
- 3 large eggs
- 3/4 cup (105 grmas) all purpose flour
- 1/4 teaspoon salt
- Chocolate Frosting:
- 4 ounces (120 grams) semi-sweet or bittersweet chocolate, chopped
- 6 tablespoons (3 ounces) (84 grams) unsalted butter, cut in pieces
- 3/4 teaspoon pure vanilla extract
- 2 teaspoons light corn syrup 1 1/3 cups (155 grams) confectioners (powder or icing) sugar, sifted
- 1/2 cup sour cream, room temperature
- 1 teaspoon hot water

Direction

- Preheat oven to 325 degrees F (170 degrees C) and place rack in centre of oven. Line 12 muffin tins with paper or foil baking cups.
- Melt the chopped chocolate and butter in a stainless steel bowl placed over a saucepan of simmering water. (The double bowler) Once the chocolate is melted and smooth, remove from heat and let cool for a few minutes. The stir (can also use a hand mixer) in the sugar. Add the vanilla and then add the eggs, one at a time, mixing well after each addiction. Mix in the flour and salt until well blended.
- Evenly divide the batter between the muffin cups. Place in the preheated oven and bake for about 20 min or until a toothpick inserted in the centre of the cupcake has moist crumbs. Remove from oven and let cool on a wire rack.

- To make Chocolate Frosting melt the chocolate and butter in a heatproof bowl placed over a saucepan of simmering water. (Again the double bowler) Remove from heat and stir in the vanilla and corn syrup. Whisk in the sugar, a little at a time (at this point the frosting will be quite thick). Place the frosting in the bowl of your food processor and, with the processor running. Gradually add the sour cream and hot water. Process until the frosting is nice and shiny. At this point you can simply spread some frosting, on the top of each cupcake. However, if you want to pipe the frosting in the fridge for it to firm up. Periodically check and stir the frosting until it is of the desired piping consistency.
- Makes 12 cupcakes.

24. Brownies Recipe

Serving: 0 | Prep: | Cook: | Ready in:

Ingredients

- 0

Direction

- 0

25. Bunny Cupcakes For Kids Of All Ages Recipe

Serving: 12 | Prep: | Cook: 25mins | Ready in:

Ingredients

- 1/4 C butter, softened
- 1 C Imperial® or Dixie Crystals® Extra Fine Granulated sugar
- 2 eggs
- 1 tsp. vanilla extract
- 1 C all-purpose flour
- 1/2 tsp. baking powder
- 1/2 tsp. baking soda
- 1/2 tsp. salt
- 2 one-ounce squares unsweetened chocolate, melted and cooled
- 1/2 C sour cream
- Cream butter with sugar until light and fluffy. Add eggs, one at a time, beating well after each addition. Stir in vanilla extract. Sift flour with the baking powder, baking soda and salt and gradually stir into the creamed mixture.
- Stir in the melted and cooled chocolate and the sour cream. Spray six giant muffin cups well with a non-stick cooking spray. Divide batter evenly among the six muffin cups and bake in a preheated 350 degrees oven for 20-25 minutes or until cakes spring back if lightly pressed in the centers with your fingertips.
- Cool in the pan 5-10 minutes then turn out onto a rack to cool completely. When cool cut as directed in our diagram. Frost and decorate as desired with our Creamy Bunny frosting.
- Creamy Bunny Frosting:
- 8 oz. cream cheese, softened
- 8 C Imperial® or Dixie Crystals® powdered sugar
- 1 tsp. vanilla extract
- 5-6 T milk
- 3-4 T all-purpose flour
- Tiny jellybeans (for decorating)
- Pink construction paper (for ears)
- Beat cream cheese until light and fluffy. Add powdered sugar and blend well; mixture will be crumbly. Add vanilla extract and milk, one tablespoon at a time to desired consistency. Add flour and blend until smooth. "Glue" body parts together with a small amount of frosting. Then frost bunny and add decorations.

Direction

- To Cut and Form Bunnies:
- Slice each cupcake in half horizontally forming two circles, (each cupcake forms two bunnies by the way). Slice each circle in half, forming 4

semicircles. Stand two semicircles together, rounded edge up.
- Glue these two semicircles together with a small amount of frosting. Then glue the remaining two semicircles together in the same fashion.
- Now, cut a small wedge from one end of the glued semicircle. Save one half of the wedge for the bunny's tail. Pop other half of the wedge into your mouth. It's good, isn't it?
- Glue the bunny tail onto the rounded end of the standing semicircles. Frost and decorate.
- Decorating Ideas for Bunny Cupcakes for Kids:
- Cut bunny ears from a sheet of pink construction paper. Make a small fold in the base of each ear to give the ear a sense of realistic depth.
- Pat shredded coconut onto each bunny while the frosting is still 'wet' to give your bunnies white 'fur'.
- Tint some frosting with food colouring and pipe eyes and noses onto bunnies or pipe a small flower under each bunny's nose!
- Serve bunnies on small individual plates surrounded by shredded coconut that has been tinted green (optional)

26. Bunny Cupcakes Recipe

Serving: 12 | Prep: | Cook: | Ready in:

Ingredients

- Cupcakes (baked from your favorite recipe)
- White icing (I have a recipe)
- shredded coconut
- Pink decorators' sugar
- jelly bean nose
- Chewable Sweet Tart eyes
- Large marshmallow
- mini marshmallows

Direction

- Frost a cupcake with white icing and sprinkle on shredded coconut fur.
- Cut a large marshmallow in half width wise. Squeeze each half slightly to give it an oval shape, then decorate the sticky side of each one with pink decorators' sugar and set them in place for ears.
- Add a jelly bean nose and either jelly bean or snipped Sweet Tart eyes, and mini marshmallows for cheeks. For a finishing touch, draw on decorators' gel pupils or whiskers if you like.

27. Buttermilk Chocolate Cupcakes Recipe

Serving: 24 | Prep: | Cook: 30mins | Ready in:

Ingredients

- 1/2 cup butter, softened
- 1-1/2 cups sugar
- 2 eggs
- 1 teaspoon vanilla extract
- 1-1/2 cups all-purpose flour
- 1/2 cup baking cocoa
- 1 teaspoon baking soda
- 1/4 teaspoon salt
- 1/2 cup buttermilk
- 1/2 cup water
- FROSTING:
- 1/2 cup butter, softened
- 3-3/4 cups confectioners' sugar
- 2 squares (1 ounce each) unsweetened chocolate, melted
- 2 tablespoons evaporated milk
- 1 teaspoon vanilla extract
- 1/4 teaspoon salt
- chocolate sprinkles

Direction

- In a large mixing bowl, cream butter and sugar until light and fluffy.

- Add eggs, one at a time, beating well after each addition.
- Beat in vanilla.
- Combine the flour, cocoa, baking soda and salt.
- Add dry ingredients to creamed mixture alternately with buttermilk mixture, beating well after each addition.
- Fill paper-lined muffin cups two-thirds full.
- Bake at 375° for 15-20 minutes or until a toothpick comes out clean. Cool for 10 minutes before removing from pans to wire racks to cool completely.
- For frosting, in a small mixing bowl, beat butter and confectioners' sugar until smooth.
- Beat in the melted chocolate, milk, vanilla and salt.
- Frost cupcakes; garnish with chocolate sprinkles.
- Yield: 2 dozen.

28. Buttermilk Iced Pumpkin Cupcakes Recipe

Serving: 30 | Prep: | Cook: 20mins | Ready in:

Ingredients

- 4 cups cake flour
- 1 tablespoon plus 1 teaspoon baking powder
- 2 1/4 teaspoons ground cinnamon
- 2 1/4 teaspoons ground ginger
- 1 teaspoon ground cloves
- 1 teaspoon freshly grated nutmeg
- 1 teaspoon kosher salt
- 1/2 teaspoon baking soda
- 2 cups canned pumpkin purée
- 1 cup whole milk
- 2 sticks (8 ounces) unsalted butter, at room temperature
- 2 cups packed light brown sugar
- 4 large eggs, at room temperature
- 2 teaspoons vanilla extract
- ----
- buttermilk ICING:
- -----
- 1 c. firmly packed brown sugar
- 1/2 tsp. soda
- 1/4 c. butter
- 1 tbsp. corn syrup
- 1/2 c. buttermilk
- 1/2 tsp. vanilla extract
- Combine all ingredients except vanilla in saucepan. Cook about 5 minutes, stirring constantly. Remove from heat; add vanilla and beat well.

Direction

- Heat the oven to 350°F and arrange the rack in the middle.
- Line muffin pans with cupcake liners.
- Sift together dry ingredients in a bowl and set aside.
- Whisk together pumpkin and milk in a separate bowl and set aside. In the bowl of a stand mixer fitted with a paddle attachment, beat butter and sugar on high speed until light and fluffy, about 5 minutes.
- Add eggs one at a time, beating and then scraping the bowl down after each addition.
- Add vanilla and beat until smooth. Add dry ingredients in three batches, alternating with pumpkin-milk mixture, mixing on low speed, and scraping the bowl down between additions.
- When all ingredients have been added, mix batter 30 seconds on medium-high speed until uniformly combined.
- Fill the cupcake liners 3/4 full with batter and bake until a tester inserted in cupcake centres comes out clean, about 18 to 20 minutes.
- Remove cupcakes from the oven and allow to cool 5 minutes before removing from the pans.
- Let cool completely on a rack, decorate with icing, and serve.
- That's it! Enjoy

29. Cafe Metros Chocolate Cupcakes With Coconut Filling Recipe

Serving: 18 | Prep: | Cook: 25mins | Ready in:

Ingredients

- Filling:
- 8-ounce package cream cheese, softened
- 1/3 cup granulated sugar
- 1 large egg
- 1 cup sweetened coconut flakes
- 1/8 teaspoon almond extract (optional)
- ....
- chocolate batter:
- 1½ cups all-purpose flour
- 1 cup granulated sugar
- ¼ cup baking cocoa (Hershey's is recommended)
- 1 teaspoon baking soda
- ½ teaspoon salt
- 1 cup water
- 1/3 cup vegetable oil
- 1 tablespoon white vinegar
- 1 teaspoon vanilla extract
- ....
- Garnish:
- powdered sugar for sifting

Direction

- Before starting: Preheat oven to 350 degrees. Line muffin tins with paper cups.
- To make filling: Beat together cream cheese and sugar. When smooth, beat in egg. Stir in coconut and almond extract (if using). Set aside. Leftover filling can be refrigerated at least 1 week (for another batch later).
- To make chocolate batter: Stir together flour, granulated sugar, baking cocoa, baking soda and salt. Add water, vegetable oil, white vinegar and vanilla.
- Fill paper cups a little less than half full. Top with a spoonful of coconut filling. Top again with a spoonful of chocolate batter. Bake 25 minutes, or until done.
- Sift powdered sugar over tops.
- Makes 18 cupcakes.
- ....
- This is a note from the chef:
- Note: This simple, unusual recipe looks as if it won't work. But it will. (Just please resist the temptation to tamper with the written directions.) The eggless chocolate cake is tender, thanks to the acid from the vinegar, and the cream cheese filling is sweet, but not too sweet.

30. Cappuccino Cupcakes Recipe

Serving: 24 | Prep: | Cook: 19mins | Ready in:

Ingredients

- 1 package dark chocolate cake mix
- 1 1/3 strong brewed or instant coffee at room temperature
- 1/3 cup vegetable oil or butter
- 3 large eggs
- 1 container (16 ounces vanilla frosting)
- 2 tbsp coffee liqueur
- Grated chocolate, grate half of a 3 or 4 ounce milk, dark chocolate or espresso chocolate candy bar on the large holes of a standing grater.
- chocolate covered beans(optional)
- Additional coffee liqueur(optional)

Direction

- Preheat oven to 350*. Line regular size muffin pans with paper muffin cup liners
- Beat cake mix, coffee, oil and eggs with mixer at low speed for 30 seconds. Beat at medium speed for 2 minutes.
- Spoon batter into prepared muffin cups filling 2/3 full.
- Bake 18 to 20 min or until toothpick comes out clean.
- Cool in pans for 10 minutes.
- Remove from pans and cool.

- Combine frosting and 2 tbsp. liquor in small bowl; mix well
- Before frosting, poke about 10 holes in cupcake with toothpick.
- Pour 1 to 2 tsps. liqueur over top of each cupcake, if desired.
- Frost and sprinkle with chocolate
- Garnish with chocolate-covered coffee beans, if desired.

31. Cappuccino Muffins Recipe

Serving: 12 | Prep: | Cook: 15mins | Ready in:

Ingredients

- 2 cups all-purpose flour
- 1/2 cup sugar
- 2-1/2 teaspoons baking powder
- 2 teaspoons instant espresso coffee powder (or instant coffee)
- 1/2 teaspoon salt
- 1/2 teaspoon cinnamon
- 1/4 teaspoon nutmeg
- 1 cup whole milk
- 1/2 cup butter, melted and cooled
- 1 egg, slightly beaten
- 1 teaspoon vanilla extract
- 3/4 cup semi-sweet chocolate mini-chips

Direction

- Preheat oven to 375 degrees F.
- Line muffin tins with papers or grease liberally.
- In a large bowl, whisk together flour, sugar, baking powder, espresso or instant coffee, salt, cinnamon, and nutmeg.
- Set aside.
- In a medium bowl, mix milk, butter, egg, and vanilla until combined.
- Stir milk mixture into flour mixture only until combined.
- Don't over mix.
- Fold in chocolate chips.
- Fill muffin cups 3/4 full.
- Bake 15 to 20 minutes for standard muffins, 10 to 12 minutes for mini-muffins.
- Cappuccino muffins freeze well.
- Yield: 12 muffins or about 48 mini-muffins.

32. Caramel Apple Cupcake Recipe

Serving: 9 | Prep: | Cook: 21mins | Ready in:

Ingredients

- apple Cupcakes
- 9 regular cupcakes / 350 degree oven
- 2-3 apples, Granny Smith
- 2 cups all-purpose flour
- 1/2 cup sugar
- 1 teaspoon ginger
- 1 teaspoon cinnamon
- 1/8 teaspoon nutmeg
- 1 teaspoon baking soda
- 1/4 teaspoon salt
- 2 large eggs
- 1/2 cup oil
- 1/4 cup apple juice
- 1 teaspoon vanilla
- Rinse and core the apples. Place them on an ovenproof pan or baking sheet and bake for 30-40 minutes until soft. Remove the apples from the oven, let cool slightly, then remove peel and mush the apple with the back of a fork. Measure out one cup of apple mush and set aside to cool.
- Combine flour, sugar, ginger, cinnamon, nutmeg, baking soda and salt in a medium-sized bowl and whisk to combine. Crack the eggs into a separate medium-sized bowl and beat with a fork to break up. Add the oil, apple juice, vanilla and cooled apple mush and mix to combine. Combine the wet and dry ingredients until all ingredients come together.
- Scoop into cupcake papers about 3/4 full so cupcakes will have a significant dome. Bake at 350 degrees for 20-22 minutes, rotating the pan

after 15 minutes, until a toothpick comes out clean.
- cream cheese Filling
- 1/4 stick butter
- 4 ounces Philly cream cheese
- 2 cups sifted powdered sugar
- 1 teaspoon vanilla
- Bring the butter to room temperature by letting it sit out for one or two hours. Then beat the butter vigorously with an electric mixer. Scrape the bowl and add the cream cheese and beat until combined. Add the sifted powdered sugar and vanilla. Beat until smooth.
- Thick caramel
- 1/2 cup butter
- 1 cup packed brown sugar
- 1/2 cup light corn syrup
- 6 ounces sweetened condensed milk
- 1 tablespoon heavy cream
- 1 teaspoon vanilla
- 1/2 teaspoon salt
- Bring the butter, brown sugar, corn syrup and sweetened condensed milk to a boil over medium-high heat. With a wooden spoon, stir together and then slowly add the heavy cream. Continue to stir for about 20 minutes until the caramel has reached 248 degrees. It is important to continuously stir the mixture and to allow it to reach this temperature.
- Remove from heat and stir in the vanilla and salt. Transfer to a bowl and continue to stir for two to three minutes, allowing the caramel to cool slightly.

Direction

- Assembly
- Using a small paring knife, cut a cone shape out of the top of each cupcake. Flip the cone and cut off the excess cake. Save the top for later. Fill each cavity with a teaspoon or so of cream cheese filling. Replace the top of each cupcake pressing down firmly to adhere the top to the filling.
- Using a small offset spatula, frost each cupcake with the caramel. If desired, sprinkle warm caramel with toppings, such as coconut or crushed nuts. Transfer the cupcake into the freezer to allow the caramel to set without dripping over the edge of the cupcake paper.
- Continue frosting and topping the cupcakes and try to work fast. As the caramel cools, it becomes less easy to spread. If possible, work in pairs and let your helper top the cupcakes and transfer them to the freezer. By the time you reach the last few cupcakes, you will no longer need to freeze them and you can take all the cupcakes out and transfer them to the counter.
- Top off each cupcake with a Popsicle or craft stick to finish off the look.

33. Carrot Cake W Cream Cheese Frosting Recipe

Serving: 22 | Prep: | Cook: 45mins | Ready in:

Ingredients

- 2 cups sugar
- 1 1/3 cups vegetable oil
- 1 teaspoon pure vanilla extract
- 3 extra-large eggs
- 2 cups all-purpose flour
- 2 teaspoons ground cinnamon
- 2 teaspoons baking soda
- 1 1/2 teaspoons kosher salt
- 3 cups grated carrots (less than 1 pound)
- 1 cup raisins (I omit these!)
- 1 cup chopped walnuts
- For the frosting:
- 3/4 pound cream cheese, at room temperature
- 1/2 pound unsalted butter, at room temperature
- 1 teaspoon pure vanilla extract
- 1 pound confectioners' sugar

Direction

- Preheat the oven to 350 degrees F.

- Beat the sugar, oil, and vanilla together in the bowl of an electric mixer fitted with a paddle attachment. Add the eggs, 1 at a time. In another bowl, sift together the flour, cinnamon, baking soda, and salt. With the mixer on low speed, add 1/2 of the dry ingredients to the wet ingredients. Add the grated carrots, raisins, and walnuts to the remaining flour, mix well, and add to the batter. Mix until just combined.
- Line muffin pans with paper liners. Scoop the batter into 22 muffin cups until each is 3/4 full. Bake at 400 degrees F for 10 minutes then reduce oven temperature to 350 degrees F and cook for a further 35 minutes, until a toothpick comes out clean. Cool on a rack.
- For the frosting, cream the cream cheese, butter, and vanilla in the bowl of an electric mixer fitted with a paddle attachment. Add the sugar and beat until smooth.
- When the cupcakes are cool, frost them generously and serve.

34. Carrot Mini Muffins Recipe

Serving: 24 | Prep: | Cook: 10mins | Ready in:

Ingredients

- 1/2 cup whole wheat flour
- 1/2 cup all-purpose flour
- 1/2 cup quick rolled oats
- 1/2 cup brown sugar
- 1 1/2 tsp. cinnamon
- 1 tsp. baking powder
- 1/2 tsp. baking soda
- 1/4 salt
- 3/4 cup soymilk mixed with 1 tsp. vinegar
- 1/4 cup canola oil
- 1 1/2 cups finely grated carrots (approximately 3 carrots)

Direction

- Preheat the oven to 350F or to 325F for a convection oven.
- Mix the ingredients in the order of the recipe until smooth.
- Spoon the batter into muffin cups.
- Bake for 40 minutes or for 25 minutes in a convection oven.
- Cool a few minutes for easier removal.

35. Carrot Ginger Cupcakes With Spiced Cream Cheese Recipe

Serving: 24 | Prep: | Cook: 15mins | Ready in:

Ingredients

- 1 pkg. (16-oz.) pound cake mix
- 3/4 cup shredded carrots
- 1 Tbsp. ground ginger
- 1 tsp. ground cinnamon, divided
- 1 tsp. walnut pieces, toasted
- 1 pkg. (8-oz.) cream cheese, softened
- 2 cups thawed whipped topping
- carrot candies

Direction

- Preheat the oven to 350*F.
- Prepare cake batter as per directions on pkg.
- Stir in carrots, ginger, 3/4 tsp. of the cinnamon and walnuts.
- Spoon batter into 24 paper-lined medium muffin cups.
- Bake 15 minutes or until toothpick comes out clean.
- Beat cream cheese in medium bowl with wire whisk until smooth.
- Gently stir in whipped topping.
- Spread over tops of cupcakes.
- Sprinkle with reserved 1/4 tsp. cinnamon
- Top with 1 carrot candy on each cupcake.
- Refrigerate until ready to serve.

36. Chai Latte Cupcakes Recipe

Serving: 24 | Prep: | Cook: 23mins | Ready in:

Ingredients

- cake
- -------
- 1 box Betty Crocker® SuperMoist® French vanilla cake mix
- 1 1/2 cups water
- 1/3 cup vegetable oil
- 3 eggs
- 1 package (1.1 oz) instant chai tea latte mix (or 3 tablespoons from larger container)
- -----------------------------
- frosting and Garnish
- -----------------------------
- 1 cup white vanilla baking chips
- 1 container (1 lb) Betty Crocker® Rich & Creamy vanilla frosting
- ground cinnamon, if desired

Direction

- Heat oven to 350°F for shiny metal pans (or 325°F for dark or non-stick pans). Place paper baking cup in each of 24 regular-size muffin cups.
- In large bowl, beat cake ingredients with electric mixer on low speed 30 seconds. Beat on medium speed 2 minutes, scraping bowl occasionally. Divide batter evenly among muffin cups.
- Bake 18 to 23 minutes or until toothpick inserted in centre comes out clean. Cool 10 minutes; remove from pan to cooling rack. Cool completely, about 1 hour.

37. Cheesecake Cookie Cups Recipe

Serving: 24 | Prep: | Cook: 25mins | Ready in:

Ingredients

- COOLING TIME: 1 HOUR
- 1 pkg. (16.5 oz.) NESTLÉ® TOLL HOUSE® Refrigerated chocolate chip Cookie Bar Dough
- 2 pkgs. (8 oz. each) cream cheese, room temperature
- 1 can (14 oz.) NESTLÉ® CARNATION® sweetened condensed milk
- 2 large eggs
- 2 teaspoons vanilla extract
- 1 can (21 oz.) cherry pie filling

Direction

- PREHEAT oven to 325° F. Paper-line 24 muffin cups. Place one piece of cookie dough in each muffin cup.

38. Chip Lovers Cupcakes Recipe

Serving: 18 | Prep: | Cook: 22mins | Ready in:

Ingredients

- 1 package (18-1/4 ounces) white cake mix
- 1/4 cup butter, softened
- 1/4 cup packed brown sugar
- 2 tablespoons sugar
- 1/3 cup all-purpose flour
- 1/4 cup confectioners' sugar
- 1/4 cup miniature semisweet chocolate chips
- butterCREAM FROSTING:
- 1/2 cup butter, softened
- 1/2 cup shortening
- 4-1/2 cups confectioners' sugar
- 4 tablespoons milk, divided
- 1-1/2 teaspoons vanilla extract
- 1/4 cup baking cocoa
- 18 miniature chocolate chip cookies

Direction

- Directions:
- Prepare cake batter according to package directions; set aside.

- For filling, in a small bowl, cream butter and sugars until light and fluffy.
- Gradually beat in flour and confectioners' sugar until blended.
- Fold in chocolate chips.
- Fill paper-lined muffin cups half full with cake batter.
- Drop filling by tablespoonfuls into the centre of each; cover with remaining batter.
- Bake at 350° for 20-22 minutes or until a toothpick inserted in cake comes out clean.
- Cool for 10 minutes before removing from pans to wire racks to cool completely.
- For frosting, in a large bowl, cream the butter, shortening and confectioners' sugar until smooth.
- Beat in 3 tablespoons milk and vanilla until creamy.
- Set aside 1 cup frosting; frost cupcakes with remaining frosting.
- Stir baking cocoa and remaining milk into reserved frosting.
- Cut a small hole in a corner of a pastry or plastic bag; insert star tip.
- Fill bag with chocolate frosting.
- Pipe a rosette on top of each cupcake; garnish with a cookie.
- Yield: 1-1/2 dozen.

39. Chipper Carrot Cupcakes Recipe

Serving: 24 | Prep: | Cook: 22mins | Ready in:

Ingredients

- 2 1/2 tbsp ground flaxseed
- 1/3 cup boiling water
- 1 cup whole wheat flour
- 2 cups flour
- 1 tsp salt
- 1 tsp baking soda
- 1/2 tsp baking powder
- 1 tbsp ground cinnamon
- 1 egg
- 2/3 cup white sugar
- 1/2 cup brown sugar, packed
- 2/3 cup canola oil
- 1 1/2 tbsp vanilla
- 3 cups grated carrot
- 2/3 cup mini chocolate chips

Direction

- Preheat oven to 350 F, and grease 24 muffin cups.
- Mix together flaxseed and water, let stand 15 minutes.
- Combine flours, salt, baking soda, baking powder and cinnamon. Set aside.
- In a large mixing bowl, beat egg, flax mixture and sugars together.
- Add oil, vanilla and carrots and blend well, scraping bowl occasionally.
- Add 1/2 the flour mixture and mix on low speed.
- Scrape down the bowl, and add the remaining flour.
- Beat just until blended.
- Fold in chocolate chips.
- Fill prepared muffin cups 3/4 full.
- Bake at 350 degrees for 20-22 minutes
- Let sit on cooling racks for 5 minutes before removing cupcakes from pans.
- Cool completely before frosting if desired.

40. Choco Raspberry Decadence Recipe

Serving: 12 | Prep: | Cook: 15mins | Ready in:

Ingredients

- ¾ cup bittersweet chocolate chips
- 2 tbsp margarine
- 2 tbsp skim milk
- 1/3 cup Splenda granular
- ½ cup unsweetened cocoa powder, sifted

- 1 egg
- 2 egg whites
- ½ cup raspberries (fresh or frozen)

Direction

- Position rack in middle of oven and preheat to 375 degrees F. Line 12-cup muffin pan with paper or foil liners.
- Heat chocolate, margarine and milk in a saucepan over low heat until melted, stirring. Remove from heat.
- Mix Splenda and cocoa. Add eggs and whisk until combined. Whisk in chocolate mixture.
- Scoop batter into muffin cups, press 3 raspberries halfway into each, and place pan on baking sheet. Bake about 15 minutes, turning front to back halfway through. Cool on rack and serve.

41. Chocolate Buttermilk Cupcakes Recipe

Serving: 24 | Prep: | Cook: 20mins | Ready in:

Ingredients

- 2 cups all-purpose flour
- 1 tsp baking soda
- 1 cup (2 sticks) unsalted butter, softened
- 1 cup granulated sugar
- 1 cup firmly-packed light brown sugar
- 4 large eggs, room temp
- 6 oz unsweetened chocolate, melted
- 1 cup buttermilk
- 1 tsp vanilla extract

Direction

- Preheat oven to 350F. Line muffin tins with paper liners.
- In a small bowl, sift together flour and baking soda. Set aside.
- In a large bowl, on medium speed of your mixer, cream butter until smooth. Add sugars and beat until fluffy, about 3 minutes. Add eggs, one at a time, beating well after each addition. Add chocolate, mixing until well incorporated.
- Add dry ingredients in 3 parts, alternating with the buttermilk and vanilla. With each addition, beat until ingredients are incorporated but do not overbeat. Using a rubber spatula, scrape down the batter in the bowl to make sure ingredients are well blended and the batter is smooth. Carefully spoon the batter into the cupcake liners, filling them about 3/4 full.
- Bake at 350F for 20-25 minutes until the tester toothpick inserted in the centre comes out clean. Cool in the tins for 15 minutes before removing them from the tins and cool completely on cooling racks before frosting.

42. Chocolate Candy Cane Cupcakes Recipe

Serving: 30 | Prep: | Cook: 23mins | Ready in:

Ingredients

- 5 squares BAKER'S Semi-sweet chocolate, divided 1 pkg. (2-layer size) chocolate cake mix 1 pkg. (3.9 oz.) JELL-O chocolate instant pudding 4 eggs 1 cup BREAKSTONE'S or KNUDSEN sour cream 1/2 cup oil 1/2 cup water 6 small candy canes, crushed, divided 1 tub (8 oz.) Cool Whip whipped topping, thawed

Direction

- HEAT oven to 350°F. Chop 4 chocolate squares; set aside. Beat cake mix, pudding mix, eggs, sour cream, oil and water with mixer on low speed until moistened. Beat on medium speed 2 min. Stir in chopped chocolate and 2 Tbsp. candy. Spoon into 30 paper-lined 2-1/2-inch muffin cups.

- BAKE 20 to 23 min. or until toothpick inserted in centres comes out clean. Cool completely.
- FROST cupcakes with COOL WHIP. Melt remaining chocolate; drizzle over cupcakes. Top with remaining candy.

43. Chocolate Chiffon Cupcakes Recipe

Serving: 18 | Prep: | Cook: 20mins | Ready in:

Ingredients

- 2 cups sugar, divided
- 1 1/2 cups cake flour
- 2/3 cup unsweetened cocoa powder
- 2 teaspoons baking powder
- 1 teaspoon salt
- 1/2 cup vegetable oil
- 7 eggs, separated and at room temperature
- 3/4 cup cold water
- 2 teaspoons vanilla extract
- 1/2 teaspoon cream of tartar

Direction

- Heat oven to 350°F (180° C).
- Combine 1-3/4 cups sugar, flour, cocoa, baking powder, salt and baking soda in large bowl. Add oil, egg yolks, water and vanilla; beat until smooth.
- Beat egg whites and cream of tartar in extra-large bowl until soft peaks form. Gradually add remaining 1/4 cup sugar, beating until stiff peaks form. Gradually pour chocolate batter over beaten egg whites, folding with rubber spatula just until blended. Spoon into prepared cupcake cups.
- Bake for about 20 minutes or until top springs back when touched lightly. Allow to cool completely before removing from muffin tin (or you could do like me, and use freestanding cupcake cups). Fill, frost and enjoy
- Makes around 18 standard cupcakes or 36 mini cupcakes.

44. Chocolate Chocolate Chip Nut Muffins Recipe

Serving: 5 | Prep: | Cook: 25mins | Ready in:

Ingredients

- INGREDIENTS
- 2 cups all-purpose flour
- 1/2 cup unsweetened cocoa powder
- 1 1/2 cups white sugar
- 1/2 teaspoon baking soda
- 2 teaspoons baking powder
- 1/4 teaspoon salt
- 1 1/4 cups milk
- 1 egg
- 2 tablespoons vegetable oil
- 1 teaspoon vanilla extract
- 1 cup semisweet chocolate chips
- 3/4 cup chopped walnuts
- 1/3 cup whole almonds
- 4 tablespoons white sugar

Direction

- DIRECTIONS
- Preheat oven to 350 degrees F (175 degrees C). Grease muffin cups or line with paper muffin liners.
- In medium bowl, sift together flour, cocoa, sugar, baking powder, baking soda and salt. In large bowl stir in milk, egg, oil and vanilla. Mix dry ingredients to large bowl; beat well. Add chocolate chips and walnuts, stir well.
- Fill muffin cups 3/4 full. Poke almonds into tops of unbaked muffins. Sprinkle muffins with sugar.
- Bake for 20 to 25 minutes, or until toothpick inserted in center comes out clean

45. Chocolate Cream Cheese Cupcakes Recipe

Serving: 20 | Prep: | Cook: 30mins | Ready in:

Ingredients

- 1 package (8 ounces) cream cheese, softened
- 1-1/2 cups sugar, divided
- 1 egg
- 1 teaspoon salt, divided
- 1 cup (6 ounces) semisweet chocolate chips
- 1-1/2 cups all-purpose flour
- 1/4 cup baking cocoa
- 1 teaspoon baking soda
- 1 cup water
- 1/3 cup vegetable oil
- 1 tablespoon white vinegar
- FROSTING:
- 3-3/4 cups confectioners' sugar
- 3 tablespoons baking cocoa
- 1/2 cup butter, melted
- 6 tablespoons milk
- 1 teaspoon vanilla extract
- 1/3 cup chopped pecans

Direction

- For filling, in a small mixing bowl, beat cream cheese and 1/2 cup sugar until smooth.
- Beat in egg and 1/2 teaspoon salt until combined. Fold in chocolate chips; set aside.
- In a bowl, combine the flour, cocoa, baking soda, and remaining sugar and salt. In another bowl, whisk the water, oil and vinegar; stir into dry ingredients just until moistened.
- Fill paper-lined muffin cups half full with batter.
- Drop filling by heaping tablespoonfuls into the centre of each.
- Bake at 350° for 24-26 minutes or until a toothpick inserted in cake comes out clean.
- Cool for 10 minutes before removing from pans to wire racks to cool completely.
- For frosting, in a large mixing bowl, combine confectioners' sugar, cocoa, butter, milk and vanilla; beat until blended.
- Frost cupcakes; sprinkle with pecans.
- Store in the refrigerator.
- Yield: 20 cupcakes.

46. Chocolate Cupcakes Recipe

Serving: 20 | Prep: | Cook: 20mins | Ready in:

Ingredients

- 1 1/2 cups of All-Purpose flour
- 2/3 cup of baking cocoa
- 1 tsp of baking soda
- 1/2 tsp of salt
- 1 1/2 cups of Granulated sugar
- 1/2 cup of Low Fat/Calorie butter or margarine
- 1 tsp of vanilla extract
- 1 cup of Low-fat (1%) milk
- 4oz of Egg Beaters (=2 eggs)

Direction

- Preheat oven to 350
- Paper line 20 muffin cups
- Combine flour, cocoa, baking soda and salt in a small bowl.
- Beat sugar, butter, eggs and vanilla extract in a large bowl.
- Gradually beat in flower mixture alternately with milk.
- Spoon 1/4 cup of batter into each muffin cup.
- Bake 18 to 20 minutes.

47. Chocolate Cupcakes Strawberry Chocolate Ganache Vanilla Buttercream Icing Recipe

Serving: 7 | Prep: | Cook: 22mins | Ready in:

Ingredients

- chocolate Cupcakes
- ~Makes 7 regular cupcakes
- 1/4 cup (1/2 stick) butter, room temp
- 1/2 cup + 2 tablespoons sugar
- 1 large egg, room temp
- 1/4 cup + 2 tablespoons flour
- 1/4 teaspoon baking powder
- 1/8 teaspoon baking soda
- 1/8 teaspoon salt
- 1/4 cup high quality unsweetened cocoa powder (I also used Valrhona cocoa powder)
- 1/4 cup milk
- 1/2 teaspoon vanilla extract
- Strawberry Ganache Filling and Ganache glaze
- 4.5 ounces semi-sweet chocolate (I used Callebaut)
- 3/4 cup heavy cream
- 1/2 teaspoon vanilla
- pinch salt
- 1/3 cup strawberries, diced
- vanilla buttercream frosting
- 1 stick (1/2 cup) unsalted butter, room temperature
- 1 tablespoon milk
- 1 teaspoon vanilla bean paste
- 2 1/4 cups powdered sugar

Direction

- Pre-heat oven to 350 degrees F.
- 1. Beat butter until softened. Add sugar and beat until light and fluffy, about 2 minutes.
- 2 Add egg and beat until well combined.
- 3. Measure the flour, baking powder, baking soda, salt, and cocoa powder into a small sized bowl and whisk to combine.
- 4. Measure out the milk and vanilla and stir to combine
- 5. Add about a third of the dry ingredients to the butter/sugar and beat to combine. Add about a half of the milk/vanilla and beat to combine. Continue adding, alternating between dry and wet and finishing with the dry.
- 6. Scoop batter into cupcake cups about 2/3's full. Bake cupcakes for about 22-25 minutes or until a cake tester comes out clean

- Strawberry Ganache Filling and Ganache Glaze
- 1. Chop chocolate and transfer into a heat proof bowl.
- 2. Heat cream until bubbles form around the edge of the pan, pour cream over the chocolate.
- 3. Let sit for 1 minute then stir until combined.
- 4. Add vanilla and salt. Stir until combined.
- 5. Divide the ganache in two approximate equal portions. In the first portion, mix in the chopped strawberries. Transfer to the refrigerator to chill.
- 6. Leave the second portion on the counter to cool down. You want the filling to thicken up before the glaze. Once the filling is think, fill the cupcakes with it. Then glaze with the glaze.
- ***See assembly instructions below. ***
- Vanilla Bean Icing Directions:
- 1. Using an electric mixer, beat the butter at medium speed until creamy.
- 2. Add the milk, vanilla extract, and 2 cups of powdered sugar and beat at low speed, occasionally stopping to scrape the sides and bottom of the bowl, until light and fluffy. Add more powdered sugar to arrive at the consistency and sweetness you like.
- Assemble:
- 1. Fill the cupcakes with the strawberry ganache filling using the cone method.
- 2. Spoon a tablespoon of glaze on each filled cupcake and smooth.
- 3. Top with buttercream frosting and a strawberry.

48. Chocolate Cupcakes With Peanut Butter Icing Recipe

Serving: 1415 | Prep: | Cook: 20mins | Ready in:

Ingredients

- 12 tablespoons unsalted butter (1 1/2 sticks) at room temperature
- 2/3 cup granulated sugar
- 2/3 cup light brown sugar, packed
- 2 extra-large eggs at room temperature
- 2 teaspoons pure vanilla extract
- 1 cup buttermilk, shaken, at room temperature
- 1/2 cup sour cream at room temperature
- 2 tablespoons brewed coffee
- 1 3/4 cups all-purpose flour
- 1 cup good un-sweetened cocoa powder
- 1 1/2 teaspoons baking soda
- 1/2 teaspoon kosher salt
- peanut butter icing
- 1 cup confectioners' sugar
- 1 cup creamy peanut butter
- 5 tablespoons unsalted butter at room temperature
- 3/4 teaspoon pure vanilla extract
- 1/4 teaspoon salt
- 1/3 cup heavy cream

Direction

- Preheat the oven to 350 degrees. Line cupcake pans with paper liners.
- In the bowl of an electric mixer fitted with a paddle attachment, cream the butter and two sugars on high speed until light and fluffy, approximately 5 minutes. Lower the speed to medium, add the eggs one at a time, then add the vanilla and mix well. In a separate bowl, whisk together the buttermilk, sour cream, and coffee. In another bowl, sift together the flour, cocoa, baking soda, and salt. On low speed, add the buttermilk mixture and the flour mixture alternately in thirds to the mixer bowl, beginning with the buttermilk mixture and ending with the flour mixture. Mix only until blended. Fold the batter with a rubber spatula to be sure it's completely blended.
- Divide the batter among the cupcake pans (one rounded standard ice cream scoop per cup is the right amount). Bake in the middle of the oven for 20 to 25 minutes, until a toothpick comes out clean. Cool for 10 minutes, remove from the pans, and allow to cool completely before frosting.
- Peanut butter icing
- Place the confectioners' sugar, peanut butter, butter, vanilla, and salt in the bowl of an electric mixer fitted with a paddle attachment. Mix on medium-low speed until creamy, scraping down the bowl with a rubber spatula as you work. Add the cream and beat on high speed until the mixture is light and smooth.

49. Chocolate Euphoria Muffins Recipe

Serving: 12 | Prep: | Cook: 1hours | Ready in:

Ingredients

- 3 tbsp chia seed*
- 1/3 cup boiling water
- 1 cup flour
- 1/3 cup Kamut flour
- 1/3 cup rolled oats (not instant)
- 2 tbsp cocoa powder
- 1 tsp baking soda
- 1 tsp baking powder
- 1/2 tsp salt
- 5 oz semisweet chocolate
- 1/4 cup canola oil
- 1/3 cup white sugar
- 1/4 cup dark brown sugar
- 1 tbsp vanilla
- 1 cup chocolate soy milk
- 1/2 cup vanilla soy yogurt
- 1 cup mini semi-sweet chocolate chips
- 1/2 cup mini (vegan) white chocolate chips

Direction

- Preheat oven to 350°F, grease a jumbo muffin pan (or line with paper cups).
- Stir together chia seed and boiling water, set aside for 10 minutes.

- In a small bowl, whisk together flours, oats, cocoa, baking soda, baking powder and salt. Set aside.
- In a large bowl in the microwave, or over a double boiler, melt the chocolate. Remove from heat.
- Stir in the canola oil until well blended, followed by the chia seed mixture, sugars and vanilla.
- Combine the chocolate soy milk and the soy yogurt, set aside.
- Beginning and ending with the dry ingredients, alternate additions of the flour and milk mixtures, stirring to just combine.
- Fold in chocolate chips.
- Bake for 30-35 minutes, until they test done.
- *If you don't have chia seed, 1/4 cup of ground flaxseed will work just as well

50. Chocolate Mint Chip Cupcakes With Mint Swiss Meringue Buttercream Frosting Recipe

Serving: 12 | Prep: | Cook: 17mins | Ready in:

Ingredients

- CAKES:
- 1/4 cup unsalted butter, room temperature
- 3/4 cup granulated sugar
- 2 ounces unsweetened chocolate, melted
- 2 large eggs, room temperature
- 1 teaspoon peppermint extract
- 1/2 cup chocolate milk
- 1 1/2 cups all-purpose flour
- 1 teaspoon baking soda
- 6 ounces mini semi-sweet chocolate chips
- butterCREAM FROSTING: (Makes 3 cups)
- 3 egg whites
- 3/4 cup granulated sugar
- 1/2 cup unsalted butter, room temperature
- 1 teaspoon peppermint extract

Direction

- CAKES:
- Preheat oven to 350 degrees F.
- Insert liners into a medium cupcake pan.
- In large bowl cream together the butter and sugar on medium speed until light and fluffy, about 3 to 5 minutes.
- Beat in melted chocolate.
- Add eggs, peppermint extract and chocolate milk.
- Beat until creamy.
- In separate bowl combine flour and baking soda.
- Add dry ingredients into chocolate mixture and beat until well blended (DO NOT OVERBEAT!).
- Stir in chocolate chips using a spatula.
- Fill cupcake liners 2/3 to 3/4 full.
- Bake 15 to 20 minutes OR until inserted toothpick comes out clean.
- Cool cakes in pan.
- FROSTING:
- Put egg whites and sugar in double boiler over simmering water.
- Whisk constantly and cook until sugar is completely dissolved and mixture is warm.
- Pour heated egg mixture into a clean mixer bowl fitted with a whisk attachment.
- Beat egg white mixture on high speed until it forms stiff (NOT dry) peaks.
- Continue beating until fluffy and cooled, about 6 minutes.
- **It is very important to beat it for the entire six minutes.
- Switch to the paddle attachment.
- With mixer on medium low, add butter several tablespoons at a time, beating well after each addition.
- **If frosting appears soupy after the butter has been added, beat on medium high speed again until smooth, 3 to 5 minutes.
- Beat in peppermint extract.
- Reduce speed to low.
- Beat 2 minutes to eliminate air bubbles.
- Stir with rubber spatula until smooth.

51. Chocolate Peanut Butter Cupcakes Recipe

Serving: 12 | Prep: | Cook: 20mins | Ready in:

Ingredients

- Cupcakes:
- 3/4 cup unsweetened cocoa powder
- 3/4 cup flour
- 1/2 teaspoon baking powder
- 1/2 teaspoon baking soda
- 1/4 teaspoon salt
- 3/4 cup (1 1/2 sticks) butter, softened
- 1/2 cup sugar
- 1/2 cup light brown sugar, packed
- 3 eggs
- 1 teaspoon vanilla
- 1/2 cup plain yogurt
- Frosting:
- 6 tablespoons butter, softened
- 3/4 cup confectioner's sugar
- 3/4 cup smooth peanut butter
- 1/4 cup heavy cream
- Reese's mini peanut butter cups, halved

Direction

- Cupcakes:
- Preheat oven to 350 degrees. Line or lightly grease 12 muffin cups.
- In a medium bowl, sift together flour, cocoa powder, baking powder, baking soda and salt. Set aside.
- In a large bowl, cream together the sugars and butter. Add the eggs and vanilla. Stir in the flour mixture in two batches, alternating with the yogurt and beginning and ending with the flour mixture.
- Spoon the batter into prepared muffin cups. Bake for 18-20 minutes. Remove from oven and let cool on a wire rack.
- Frosting:
- Using an electric mixer, beat all ingredients until smooth.
- Frost cupcakes and top with a halved Reese's mini peanut butter cup.

52. Chocolate Ricotta Muffins Recipe

Serving: 12 | Prep: | Cook: 25mins | Ready in:

Ingredients

- 2-1/3 cups unbleached all-purpose flour
- 3/4 teaspoon salt
- 2 teaspoons baking powder
- 6 to 8 tablespoons unsweetened cocoa
- 1 cup sugar
- 1 cup semisweet chocolate chips
- 1 cup ricotta cheese
- 2 large eggs
- 1-1/3 cups milk
- 1 tablespoon vanilla extract
- 4 tablespoons (1/2 stick) unsalted butter, melted

Direction

- Preheat oven to 350 degrees.
- Lightly spray 12 standard (2-1/2-inch diameter) muffin cups with non-stick spray.
- Combine flour, salt, baking powder, cocoa, sugar and chocolate chips in a medium-sized bowl.
- Place the ricotta in a second medium-sized bowl, and add the eggs one at a time, beating well with a medium-sized whisk after each addition.
- Add the milk and vanilla, and whisk until thoroughly blended.
- Pour the ricotta mixture, along with the melted butter, into the dry ingredients.
- Using a spoon or a rubber spatula, stir from the bottom of the bowl until the dry ingredients are all moistened.
- Don't overmix; a few lumps are OK.
- Spoon the batter into the prepared muffin cups.

- For smaller muffins, fill the cups about four-fifths full.
- For larger muffins, fill them up to the top.
- If you have extra batter, spray one or two additional muffin cups with non-stick spray and fill with the remaining batter.
- Bake in the middle of the oven for 20 to 25 minutes, or until lightly browned on top and a toothpick inserted into the center comes out clean.
- Remove the pan from the oven, then remove the muffins from the pan and place them on a rack to cool.
- Wait at least 30 minutes before serving.

53. Chocolate Sour Cream Cupcakes Recipe

Serving: 1 | Prep: | Cook: 25mins | Ready in:

Ingredients

- 1/2 cup boiling water
- 1/4 cup shortening or butter
- 1 cup granulated sugar
- 1/4 cup unsweetened cocoa powder
- 1 1/2 cups all-purpose flour
- 1/2 teaspoon salt
- 1/2 teaspoon baking powder
- 1/2 teaspoon soda
- 1 egg, beaten
- 1/2 cup sour cream
- 1/2 teaspoon vanilla extract

Direction

- In a mixing bowl, combine boiling water, shortening, sugar, and cocoa. Beat until sugar is dissolved.
- Add sifted dry ingredients alternately with the beaten egg, sour cream, and vanilla.
- Fill greased and lightly floured cupcake cups about half full.
- Bake at 350° for 25 minutes. Frost with your favourite frosting,

54. Chocolate Zucchini And Carrot Cupcakes Recipe

Serving: 21 | Prep: | Cook: 22mins | Ready in:

Ingredients

- 1-1/4 cups butter, softened
- 1-1/2 cups sugar
- 2 eggs
- 1 teaspoon vanilla extract
- 2-1/2 cups all-purpose flour
- 3/4 cup baking cocoa
- 1 teaspoon baking powder
- 1 teaspoon baking soda
- 1/2 teaspoon salt
- 1/2 cup plain yogurt
- 1 cup grated zucchini
- 1 cup grated carrots
- 1 can (16 ounces) chocolate frosting

Direction

- Directions:
- In a large bowl, cream butter and sugar until light and fluffy.
- Add eggs, one at a time, beating well after each addition.
- Stir in vanilla.
- Combine the flour, baking cocoa, baking powder, baking soda and salt; add to the creamed mixture alternately with yogurt, beating well after each addition.
- Fold in zucchini and carrots.
- Fill paper-lined muffin cups two-thirds full.
- Bake at 350° for 18-22 minutes or until a toothpick comes out clean.
- Cool for 10 minutes before removing from pans to wire racks to cool completely.
- Frost cupcakes.
- Yield: 21 cupcakes.

55. Chocolate Surprise Muffins Recipe

Serving: 8 | Prep: | Cook: 12mins | Ready in:

Ingredients

- 100 grams Bittersweet chocolate; 60 % cocoa, chopped
- 100 grams butter
- 3 eggs
- 130 grams sugar + sprinkling the muffin moulds
- 1 tsp vanilla sugar
- 1 pinch salt
- 40 grams flour
- 40 grams hazelnuts, ground
- 6-8 Chocolate, diced
- 1-2 tsp icing sugar

Direction

- Preheat oven to 200 °C/400 F. Butter and sugar 6 to 8 moulds from a muffin tray. Chill.
- Stir chocolate and butter in heavy medium saucepan over low heat until melted. Cool slightly.
- Whisk eggs and sugar in large bowl until getting pale and fluffy about 5 minutes. Whisk in the chocolate mixture. Then, carefully fold in the flour and the hazelnuts. Pour batter into muffin moulds, dividing equally. Press one chocolate peace in every mould, cover with batter. Bake for 12 minutes. Remove cakes from tin and dust with icing sugar.
- The batter can be made 1 day ahead and filled into the moulds. Cover; chill.

56. Chocolaty Chocolate Chip Muffins Recipe

Serving: 48 | Prep: | Cook: 19mins | Ready in:

Ingredients

- 4 cups all-purpose flour
- 4 cups whole wheat flour
- 2 cups granulated sugar
- 2 teaspoons baking powder
- 2 tablespoons baking soda
- 2 teaspoons salt
- 8 tablespoons unsweetened cocoa powder
- 4 large eggs
- 3 1/2 cups milk
- 1 1/3 cups vegetable oil
- 3 cups semisweet chocolate morsels
- 2 teaspoons ground cinnamon
- 2 teaspoons ground nutmeg
- 1 tablespoon vanilla

Direction

- 1. Turn the oven on to 350°F.
- 2. Spray cooking spray on four 12 cup muffin pans, or four 6 cup Texas size muffin pans.
- 3. Combine both flours, cocoa, sugar, baking powder, baking soda and salt into a large mixing bowl.
- 4. Combine the milk, eggs and vegetable oil in a medium mixing bowl, add this to the flour mixture; mix it until it is moist.
- 5. Stir in 3 cups chocolate morsels and any nuts if desired. Pour into waiting cupcake pans.
- 6. Bake these at 350° F for 18-20 minutes if you are using the 12 cup pans. Bake for 22-25 minutes if using the 6 cup pans. Let cool, remove. Let cool on wire racks if desired.

57. Christmas Cupcakes Recipe

Serving: 12 | Prep: | Cook: 30mins | Ready in:

Ingredients

- 2 cups of cake flour
- 1 cup + 1 tbsp sugar
- 1/2 tsp salt
- 3 3/4 tsp baking powder
- 1/3 cup dark cocoa powder, compacted

- 1/2 butter or margarine
- 4 1/2 tsp oil
- 2 eggs
- 1 tbsp vanilla
- 1 cup milk
- Decoration:
- 5 1/2 cups of whipped cream
- 12 whole red or green candied cherres
- 12 whole green candied cherries, extra
- rainbow sprinkles
- silver dragees (balls)
- icing sugar

Direction

- Sift the cake flour twice.
- Using 2 large mixing bowls, sift together twice, flour, sugar, salt, baking powder and cocoa.
- Transfer to a medium mixing bowl.
- Add butter.
- Mix until everything is fine and crumbly like wet sand.
- Add oil, eggs, vanilla and milk.
- Mix well.
- Mix with hand mixer on high speed for 4 minutes until thick and fluffy.
- Spoon into greased muffin tins to the top.
- Bake for 26 - 27 minutes on 180 degrees.
- Let the cupcakes cool for 7 minutes before transferring to a cool rack.
- Store the cupcakes after cooling in an airtight plastic container overnight to soften the edges for cutting.
- Assembling the trees:
- Cut 12 red and 12 green cherries into quarters and then each quarter into 6 - 8 bits.
- Place in separate bowl for later use.
- Whip up the cream.
- Place cupcake upside down on a cutting surface.
- Slice off the bottom of cupcake.
- Set bottom aside.
- Take the cap and place it upright.
- Carefully slice a bit off the top to make the tree top (1st layer)
- Slice rest of the cap into two equal layers.
- Place the bottom part upright and scoop out a hole using a melon baller or knife.
- Using a pastry bag fitted with a star tip, pipe out a bit of topping into the hole.
- Insert a whole cherry.
- Pipe out topping to cover the cherry.
- Place bottom layer with top cut side facing up, over the piped topping.
- Pipe cream over it
- Repeat with other layers.
- Don't pipe anything on top yet.
- Sprinkle rainbow sprinkles all around.
- Put cut cherries all around.
- Pipe out a star on top.
- Put silver dragee on top.
- Sift some icing sugar over.

58. Cincinnati Chili Cupcakes Recipe

Serving: 12 | Prep: | Cook: 25mins | Ready in:

Ingredients

- For the cupcakes:
- 1 1/2 cups all-purpose flour
- 1 cup sugar
- 1/4 cup cocoa powder
- 1 teaspoon baking soda
- 1/2 teaspoon salt
- 1 1/2 t chile powder*
- 3/4 t ground cinnamon
- 1/4 t ground allspice
- pinch cayenne pepper
- 1/2 cup chocolate chips
- 5 tablespoons neutral vegetable oil
- 1 teaspoon vanilla extract
- 1 tablespoon vinegar (apple cider or white)
- 1 cup cold water
- *Be sure to check for other ingredients in spice jars labelled "chili powder". You want to buy pure chile powder and not anything with cumin, onion, garlic, etc added.
- For the frosting:

- 1/4 cup margarine (or butter)
- 1/4 cup shortening
- 3 cups powdered sugar
- 2 teaspoons vanilla extract
- Plus white chocolate and icing colors to decorate

Direction

- To make the cakes:
- Preheat oven to 350 degrees F and line a cupcake pan with papers.
- Add the flour, sugar, cocoa, baking powder, salt and spices to a large bowl. Stir with a wire whisk until full incorporated. Add the chocolate chips and stir to distribute.
- Mix together the oil, vanilla, vinegar and water in a small bowl. Add the wet ingredients to the dry ingredients and stir until combined. Fill the cupcake papers three quarters full.
- Bake for 20-25 minutes until a toothpick inserted into the centre of a cupcake comes out with only a few crumbs clinging.
- Cool for 5-10 minutes and then transfer the cupcakes to a wire rack to finish cooling.
- Frost and decorate.
- To make the frosting:
- Beat the margarine and shortening until smooth.
- Slowly sift in the powdered sugar and beat until light and fluffy.
- Add the vanilla extract and beat until mixed in.
- Fill a piping bag with a #4 Wilton tip or snip a very small opening to create the "spaghetti".
- To decorate:
- I made the orange "cheese" with orange colored white chocolate. I get dairy-free white chocolate from Chocolate Emporium. I melted the chocolate chips carefully in the microwave and then added both Wilton Lemon Yellow and Orange icing colours to get the ideal orange shade. I chilled the colored block of chocolate in the freezer. When I was ready to decorate, I microwaved the block of chocolate in 5 second increments to get it just warm and pliable enough to grate.

59. Cinnamon Struesel Cupcakes From The Cupcakery Recipe

Serving: 24 | Prep: | Cook: 25mins | Ready in:

Ingredients

- 1 French vanilla cake mix + ingredients listed on the box for preparing
- Topping:
- 2 C. brown sugar
- 1-1/2 tsp. cinnamon
- 1 T. dry cake mix
- Glaze:
- 1 C. powdered sugar
- 2 T. milk

Direction

- Make cake mix following box directions, reserving 1 T. of the dry mix for the topping.
- Set batter aside.
- Mix topping ingredients.
- Layer in muffin cups, starting with batter, then topping.
- Bake, according to box directions.
- Mix ingredients for glaze and top the cooled cupcakes with glaze.

60. Cinnamon Swirl Snickerdoodle Cupcakes Recipe

Serving: 12 | Prep: | Cook: 20mins | Ready in:

Ingredients

- 1 cup soymilk
- 1 teaspoon apple cider vinegar
- 1/3 cup + 2 teaspoons vegetable oil

- 1 1/4 cup flour
- 2 tablespoons cornstarch
- 3/4 teaspoon baking powder
- 1/2 teaspoon baking soda
- 1/2 teaspoon salt
- 3/4 cup sugar
- 2 teaspoons vanilla
- 1/2 teaspoon orange extract
- 2 teaspoons cinnamon
- 2 tablespoons brown sugar

Direction

- Preheat oven to 350 degrees F. Line a cupcake pan with paper liners.
- Mix together soymilk and vinegar and set aside for 1-5 minutes.
- In a separate bowl, mix together flour, cornstarch, baking powder, baking soda, salt, and white sugar.
- In a small bowl, mix together the cinnamon, brown sugar and 2 teaspoons of the vegetable oil.
- Add remaining oil and the orange and vanilla extracts to the soured soymilk. Stir together and add to the dry ingredients. Mix together to form a smooth batter. Pour into the lined cupcake pan, filling each cup no more than 2/3 full.
- Spoon a heaping 1/2 teaspoon full of the cinnamon mixture into each cupcake. Make a zigzag or spiral in the cupcake batter with a bamboo stick or toothpick.
- Bake for 19-22 minutes until a toothpick inserted in the centre comes out clean.
- Allow to cool and frost with vanilla frosting and sprinkle with cinnamon sugar.
- Frosting Notes: I rarely measure when I make vanilla frosting. I just take 1/2 cup of softened Earth Balance and 1 teaspoon of vanilla extract and beat it with enough sifted powdered sugar to get the right consistency and taste. If it gets too thick I think it with a little soy milk.

61. Cinnamon Vanilla Buttercream Frosting Recipe

Serving: 12 | Prep: | Cook: | Ready in:

Ingredients

- 1 cup (2 sticks) unsalted butter, softened
- 6 to 8 cups confectioners' sugar
- 1/2 cup milk
- 2 teaspoons vanilla extract
- 2 teaspoons cinnamon
- or replace last 2 ing. with
- 3tsp lemon/lime juice
- or 3tsp dried ginger
- or try any extract you fancy........

Direction

- In a food processor, mix up the butter.
- Add half the amount of sugar, and pulse again.
- Pour in the rest of the sugar, milk, extract, and cinnamon. Pulse until completely mixed.
- Pop in fridge for about five minutes,
- Fill the piper and decorate.

62. Cocoa Velvet Cupcakes Recipe

Serving: 4 | Prep: | Cook: 25mins | Ready in:

Ingredients

- 4 cups sugar
- 1 pound (4 sticks) butter
- 4 eggs
- 3/4 cup cocoa powder
- 1 tube of red food coloring, if you want to make an effort
- 5 cups flour
- 2 teaspoons salt
- 2 cups buttermilk
- 4 teaspoons vanilla extract
- 1 teaspoon baking soda
- 2 tablespoons vinegar

Direction

- Preheat oven to 350°F.
- Prep a bunch of cupcake tins by greasing or with paper liners.
- In a large mixing bowl, cream the sugar and butter.
- Add the eggs one at a time and mix well after each addition.
- Add the cocoa and food colouring to the bowl.
- Sift together flour and salt.
- Add flour mixture to the creamed mixture alternately with buttermilk.
- Blend in vanilla.
- In a small bowl, combine baking soda and vinegar and add to mixture. (This is fun! A la second grade science experiments.)
- Pour batter into cupcake liners.
- Bake for 20 to 25 minutes.
- If so inclined, put in freezer for half an hour to cool. This gives them the slightly denser, fudgy texture that I happen to like.
- Frost with icing of your choice. I used the not-too-sweet Creamy Vanilla Cream Cheese Icing">Creamy Vanilla Cream Cheese Icing. I topped with nonpareils and slightly icky but pretty Boston Baked Bean candied peanuts.

63. Coconut Chocolate Chip Cupcakes Cupcakes Recipe

Serving: 20 | Prep: | Cook: 22mins | Ready in:

Ingredients

- 1 cup whole wheat pastry flour
- 1 cup unbleached all purpose flour
- 1/2 cup coconut milk powder (sifted, then measured)
- 1 teaspoon baking powder
- 1/2 teaspoon salt
- 1 1/4 cups (2 1/2 sticks) unsalted butter, room temperature
- 1 3-ounce package cream cheese, room temperature
- 1 1/2 cups sugar
- 1/2 teaspoon vanilla extract
- 4 drops coconut flavoring or 3/4 teaspoon coconut extract
- 5 large eggs
- 2 tablespoons whole milk
- 1 3/4 cups bittersweet chocolate chips (10 to 11 ounces)
- Frosting:
- 1/2 cup (1 stick) unsalted butter, room temperature
- 1/2 cup coconut milk powder (sifted, then measured)
- 1/4 teaspoon salt
- 1/2 teaspoon vanilla extract
- 3 drops coconut flavoring or 1/2 teaspoon coconut extract
- 4 to 5 cups powdered sugar (16 to 20 ounces)
- 4 tablespoons (or more) whole milk
- Flaked sweetened coconut (optional)
- INGREDIENT TIP:
- coconut milk powder is simply evaporated unsweetened coconut milk. In these cupcakes, it adds subtle flavor and luscious texture. Look for it at specialty foods stores, Asian markets, and online at kingarthurflour.com and amazon.com.

Direction

- For cupcakes:
- Preheat oven to 350°F. Line 20 standard (1/3-cup) muffin cups with paper liners. Sift first 5 ingredients into medium bowl. Using electric mixer, beat butter and cream cheese in large bowl until smooth. Gradually beat in sugar, then vanilla extract and coconut flavouring. Beat in dry ingredients (batter will be stiff). Add eggs 1 at a time, beating to blend after each addition. Beat in milk, then stir in chocolate chips. Spoon scant 1/3 cup batter into each paper liner. Bake cupcakes until tester inserted into centres comes out clean, about 22 minutes. Let cool 10 minutes, then turn cupcakes out of pan and cool on rack.

- For frosting:
- Using electric mixer, beat butter, coconut milk powder, and salt in large bowl until smooth. Beat in vanilla extract and coconut flavouring. Beat in enough powdered sugar, 1 cup at a time, to form very thick frosting. Beat in milk, 1 tablespoon at a time, until frosting is thin enough to spread.
- Spread frosting on cupcakes. Sprinkle with flaked coconut, if desired. DO AHEAD: Can be made 1 day ahead. Store cupcakes airtight at room temperature.

64. Cone A Cake Recipe

Serving: 14 | Prep: | Cook: 20mins | Ready in:

Ingredients

- 1 pkg. Jiffy cake mix
- 14 flat bottom ice cream cones

Direction

- Prepare cake mix per package directions.
- Pour a scant 1/4 cup batter into each of the 14 cones, filling to just less than 1/2 full. If the cones are filled more than that the batter will run over the top.
- Stand cones upright in muffin tins.
- Bake at 350 degrees for 15 to 20 minutes.
- Cool, frost and decorate as desired.

65. Copycat Starbucks Black Bottom Cupcakes Recipe

Serving: 36 | Prep: | Cook: 50mins | Ready in:

Ingredients

- ***Filling:***
- 8 ounces cream cheese, room temp
- 1/3 cup sugar
- 1 large egg
- dash salt
- 1 small bag milk chocolate chips
- ***cake Batter:***
- 2/3 cup cocoa
- 3 cups flour
- 2 cups sugar
- 2 teaspoons baking soda
- 1/2 teaspoon salt
- 2 cups water
- 2/3 cup oil
- 2 tablespoons vinegar
- 2 teaspoons vanilla

Direction

- Preheat oven to 350 degrees.
- Cream the sugar and cream cheese. Mix in the egg and salt. Now stir in chocolate chips. Set the filling aside.
- Sift together flour, sugar, cocoa, baking soda, and salt. Next add water, oil, vinegar and vanilla. Mix well.
- Fill cupcake liners a little more than half full with chocolate batter. Drop about a generous teaspoon of cream cheese mixture on the top of each in the middle.
- Bake in a 350 degree oven for approximately 20 minutes. About 10 minutes into baking, sprinkle some extra chocolate chips on top of each cupcake.
- Makes three dozen.

66. Cotton Candy Cupcakes For Kids Recipe

Serving: 24 | Prep: | Cook: 18mins | Ready in:

Ingredients

- CUPCAKES:
- 1pkg. (18.25oz.) white cake mix
- 1-1/2c. blueberry yogurt (2-6oz. containers)
- 1/4c. water

- 1/4c. vegetable oil
- 3 egg whites (you can use the whole egg, however the batter will be more green rather than blue.)
- 5-6 drops blue food coloring
- COTTON CANDY BUTTERCREAM:
- 3oz. blue cotton candy (4c.); divided
- 4T. butter; softened
- 3c. powdered sugar; sifted
- 3T. milk

Direction

- Line baking cups with paper liners.
- Preheat oven to 350F.
- Blend all cupcake ingredients on low speed of mixer for 30 sec. & then med. speed for 2 min.
- Fill cups 2/3 full with the batter.
- Bake cupcakes 17-20 min. Cool before frosting.
- Frost with Cotton Candy Buttercream & garnish with fluffs of Cotton Candy.
- COTTON CANDY BUTTERCREAM:
- Blend butter in mixing bowl 30sec. or until creamy.
- Add 2-1/2c. Cotton candy & beat until incorporated. (The mixture will be blue & grainy).
- Add confectioner's sugar and milk & blend on low until frosting comes together & is nearly smooth, approx. 1-1/2 min. (It will still be slightly grainy).
- Increase speed to med. high & beat for 30sec. to incorporate air so that frosting will be fluffy.
- NOTE: The cotton candy will harden @ room temperature, so keep the cupcakes in a cake saver or under a glass dome.

67. Cream Cheese Chocolate Cupcakes Recipe

Serving: 18 | Prep: | Cook: 25mins | Ready in:

Ingredients

- Filling:
- 1 package (8 oz.) cream cheese, softened
- 1/3 c. sugar
- 1 egg
- 1/8 tsp. salt
- 1 c. chocolate chips
- 1 c. peanut butter chips (or just use more chocolate if you want)
- Cupcakes:
- 1 1/2 c. all-purpose flour
- 1 c. sugar
- 1/4 c. baking cocoa
- 1 tsp. baking soda
- 1/2 tsp. salt
- 1 c. water
- 1/3 c. vegetable oil
- 1 Tbs. white vinegar
- 1 tsp. vanilla

Direction

- In a bowl, beat cream cheese. Add sugar, egg, salt. Mix well. Fold in chips. Set aside.
- For cupcakes, combine flour, sugar, cocoa, baking soda, and salt.
- Add water, oil, vinegar, and vanilla. Mix well.
- Fill paper-lined muffin cups half full with batter. Top each with 2 Tbs. of cream cheese mixture.
- Bake at 350º for 25-30 minutes.
- Cool 10 minutes and remove from pan.

68. Cream Cheese Cupcakes Recipe

Serving: 12 | Prep: | Cook: 25mins | Ready in:

Ingredients

- 1 3 Oz. Pkg. cream cheese, softened
- 1 yellow cake mix
- 1 ¼ Cups water
- ½ Cup butter, melted
- 3 eggs
- chocolate frosting, optional

Direction

- In a large mixing bowl, beat cream cheese until smooth. Beat in cake mix, water, butter and eggs.
- Spoon batter into paper-lined muffin cups.
- Bake at 350 degrees for 25 minutes or until golden brown.
- Remove to a wire rack to cool completely. Frost with Chocolate Frosting or maybe Cream Cheese Icing.

69. Cream Filled Chocolate Cupcakes Recipe

Serving: 12 | Prep: | Cook: 30mins | Ready in:

Ingredients

- FOR THE CUPCAKES
- 1 cup (2 sticks) unsalted butter, room temperature, plus more for muffin tins
- 3/4 cup unsweetened cocoa powder, plus more for muffin tins
- 2 cups all-purpose flour (spooned and leveled)
- 2 teaspoons baking powder
- 1/2 teaspoon baking soda
- 1/2 teaspoon salt
- 2 cups sugar
- 3 large eggs, room temperature
- 1 cup sour cream, room temperature
- FOR THE FILLING
- 1 1/2 cups marshmallow creme (7.5-ounce jar)
- 1/2 cup (1 stick) unsalted butter, room temperature

Direction

- Preheat oven to 350. Butter two 6-cup (each with a 1-cup capacity) jumbo muffin pans; dust with cocoa powder to coat, tapping out excess. In a medium bowl, whisk together cocoa, flour, baking powder, soda, and salt.
- Using an electric mixer, beat butter and sugar until light. Add eggs one at a time, beating well after each addition. On low speed, add half the flour mixture, followed by sour cream, ending with remaining flour mixture; mix just until incorporated (do not over mix).
- Divide batter among prepared muffin cups. Bake until a toothpick inserted in centre of a cupcake comes out clean, 25 to 30 minutes, rotating pans halfway through baking. Cool in pans, 5 minutes; remove cupcakes and cool, right side up, on a wire rack.
- Meanwhile, prepare filling: In a medium bowl, whisk marshmallow crème and butter until smooth. Chill until slightly firm, 15 to 30 minutes. Transfer mixture to a heavy-duty resealable plastic bag, and seal; cut off one corner of the bag to make a 1/8-inch opening.
- Using a small melon baller, scoop out centre of each cupcake from the bottom, and reserve (you will use this to plug cupcake after filling). Hollow out each cupcake a bit more, discarding crumbs. Insert tip of plastic bag into each cavity, and squeeze to fill; replace plugs. Using remaining filling in plastic bag, decorate top of cupcakes.

70. Cream Filled Cupcakes Recipe

Serving: 24 | Prep: | Cook: 15mins | Ready in:

Ingredients

- 1 package (18-1/4 oz.) devil's food cake mix
- ************************************
- 2 tsp. hot water
- 1/4 tsp. salt
- 1 jar (7 oz.) marshmallow creme
- 1/2 c. shortening
- 1/3 c. powdered sugar
- 1/2 tsp. pure vanilla extract
- ************************************
- Ganache frosting:
- 1 c. (6 oz.) semisweet chocolate chips
- 3/4 c. heavy whipping cream

Direction

- Prepare and bake cupcakes according to package directions for cupcakes.
- Cool for 5 min. before removing to wire racks to cool completely.
- For filling, in a small bowl, combine water and salt until salt is dissolved.
- Cool.
- In a small bowl, beat the marshmallow crème, shortening, powdered sugar and vanilla until light and fluffy; add the salt mixture.
- Cut a small hole in the corner of a pastry or plastic bag; insert round pastry tip.
- Fill the bag with cream filling.
- Push the tip through the bottom of paper cupcake liner to fill each cupcake (I filled the cupcakes through the top of them).
- In a heavy saucepan, melt the chocolate chips with cream; stir until smooth.
- Cool.
- Dip cupcake tops into frosting; chill for 20 min. or until set.
- Store in the refrigerator.
- Enjoy! :)

71. Cream Filled Chocolate Cupcakes Recipe

Serving: 24 | Prep: | Cook: 25mins | Ready in:

Ingredients

- 1 3/4 cups all-purpose flour
- 2 teaspoons baking soda
- 2 teaspoons baking powder
- 1/4 teaspoon salt
- 1 3/4 cups granulated sugar
- 4 ounces unsweetened chocolate, chopped
- 1 stick butter, cut into pieces
- 2 teaspoons vanilla extract
- 2 large eggs, slightly beaten
- **************************************
- Filling ingredients:
- **************************************
- 4 tablespoons butter, room temperature
- 1 cup powdered sugar
- 2 teaspoons vanilla extract
- 3 tablespoons heavy cream
- 1 cup marshmallow creme
- **************************************
- Ganache and icing ingredients:
- **************************************
- 6 ounces bittersweet chocolate, chopped
- 1/2 cup heavy cream
- 1 stick plus 1 tablespoon butter
- 2 1/4 teaspoons vanilla extract
- 1 tablespoon milk
- 2 cups powdered sugar

Direction

- Preheat oven to 350F degrees.
- Place paper liners in two 12-cup muffin pans.
- Prepare cupcakes by sifting together flour, baking soda, baking powder and salt in bowl.
- Bring sugar and 1 cup water to boil in saucepan, stirring until sugar dissolves.
- Pour into large bowl and add chocolate and butter.
- Let sit, stirring occasionally, until chocolate is melted and mixture has cooled slightly.
- Stir in vanilla. Using mixer, beat in eggs.
- Then mix in dry ingredients.
- Divide the batter evenly between the prepared pans and bake until toothpick inserted in centre comes out clean (about 25 minutes). Cool in pans for 25 minutes more.
- Then transfer to rack to cool completely.
- Meanwhile, prepare filling.
- Using mixer, cream butter until light and fluffy.
- Beat in 1/2 cup powdered sugar.
- Add vanilla and 1 tablespoon heavy cream.
- Beat until smooth.
- Beat in remaining powdered sugar and 2 tablespoons heavy cream in batches, alternating after each addition.
- Beat in marshmallow crème, then set aside.
- Prepare ganache by placing chocolate in a stainless steel bowl. Heat cream and 1 tablespoon butter until just boiling, then pour over the chocolate.

- Let stand for 5 minutes. Whisk until smooth, then add 2 teaspoons vanilla.
- Let stand until cool, but still glossy and liquid.
- Spoon filling into pastry bag with medium tip.
- Insert tip into centre of each cupcake top.
- Fill until the cupcake is heavier, being careful not to overfill.
- Dip the cupcake tops in the ganache.
- Chill for at least 15 minutes.
- Meanwhile, prepare icing with mixer.
- Beat remaining 1 stick butter, 1/4 teaspoon vanilla, milk and powdered sugar until smooth.
- Spoon into pastry bag with small tip.
- Pipe onto cupcakes to decorate.

72. Creamy Lime Meringue Cupcakes Recipe

Serving: 12 | Prep: | Cook: 51mins | Ready in:

Ingredients

- 1 cup flour
- 1 cup whole wheat flour
- 1/2 tsp baking powder
- 1/2 tsp baking soda
- 1/2 tsp salt
- 2/3 cup sugar
- 1/2 cup salted butter, room temperature
- 1 cup ricotta cheese, smooth
- 2 egg yolks, beaten
- 1 tbsp lime zest
- 1 tbsp lime juice
- 2 tbsp shredded coconut
- --- frosting ---
- 2 egg whites, at room temperature
- 1 cup sugar
- 1 tbsp fresh lime zest
- 1 tbsp lime juice

Direction

- Preheat the oven to 350F, line 12 muffin cups.
- In a medium bowl, whisk flours, baking powder, baking soda, and salt.
- In a large mixing bowl, cream sugar and butter until fluffy.
- Add cheese, yolks, lime zest and juice.
- Add the dry ingredients and stir until blended. Fold in the coconut.
- Bake for 20 minutes. Cool completely before frosting.
- --Frosting--
- In a large bowl, beat the egg whites until soft peaks form.
- Continue beating, at medium speed, adding sugar slowly.
- Continue whipping 5 minutes, until thick and glossy.
- Beat in the lime zest and juice.
- Preheat the broiler.
- Spread the meringue on cooled cupcakes. Place on a baking sheet and broil for 30 seconds.

73. Cupcake Pops Recipe

Serving: 0 | Prep: | Cook: | Ready in:

Ingredients

- Go to http://www.bakerella.blogspot.com/
- Scroll about 1/3 of the way down and you'll see the cupcake pops recipe

Direction

- I'm sorry for posting this way but I just had to share! :)

74. Cupcakes Three Ways Vanilla Cupcakes With Chocolate Buttercream And Rasberry Frostings Recipe

Serving: 12 | Prep: | Cook: 20mins | Ready in:

Ingredients

- 8 tablespoons (1 stick) unsalted butter, room temperature, plus more for pan
- 1 3/4 cups all-purpose flour (spooned and leveled), plus more for pan
- 2 teaspoons baking powder
- 1/2 teaspoon salt
- 3/4 cup sugar
- 2 large eggs, room temperature
- 1 teaspoon pure vanilla extract
- 1/2 cup whole milk
- vanilla, raspberry, or chocolate buttercream

Direction

- Chocolate Cupcakes
- Reduce Flour to 1 1/4 cups, and add 1/2 cup unsweetened cocoa powder. Makes 12.
- Black-and-White Cupcakes
- Prepare both vanilla and chocolate batters; fill muffin cups with 3 tablespoons of each, side by side. Makes 24.
- Preheat oven to 350 degrees. Butter and flour a standard 12-cup muffin pan, or use paper liners. In a medium bowl, whisk together flour, baking powder, and salt; set aside.
- With an electric mixer, beat butter and sugar until light and fluffy. Add eggs one at a time, beating well after each addition; add vanilla, and mix until combined. On low speed, beat in half the flour mixture, followed by milk; end with remaining flour mixture. Mix just until incorporated (do not over mix).
- Divide batter among prepared muffin cups, filling each 2/3 full. Bake until a toothpick inserted in centre of a cupcake comes out clean, 22 to 24 minutes. Cool cupcakes in pan, 5 minutes; transfer to a wire rack to cool completely. Frost with your choice of buttercream.
- Buttercream Three Ways
- Vanilla Buttercream
- With an electric mixer, beat 8 tablespoons (1 stick) room-temperature unsalted butter until light and fluffy. On medium speed, beat in 1 1/2 cups confectioners' sugar, 1/2 cup at a time, beating well after each addition and scraping down bowl as necessary. Mix in 1/2 teaspoon pure vanilla extract. Increase speed to high, and beat until light and fluffy, about 5 minutes. Makes 1 1/2 cups.
- Raspberry Buttercream
- Make Vanilla Buttercream, then beat in 3 to 4 teaspoons seedless raspberry jam.
- Chocolate Buttercream
- Place 4 ounces bittersweet chocolate in a large heatproof bowl set over (not in) a saucepan of simmering water. Heat, stirring occasionally, until smooth, 2 to 3 minutes. Remove from heat, and cool to room temperature. Make Vanilla Buttercream, then beat in melted chocolate.

75. Dark Chocolate Cupcakes With Peanut Butter Filling Recipe

Serving: 24 | Prep: | Cook: 20mins | Ready in:

Ingredients

- 3/4 cup plus 2 tablespoons cocoa powder (not Dutch process)
- 1/2 cup boiling water
- 1 cup buttermilk
- 1 3/4 cups all-purpose flour
- 1 1/4 teaspoons baking soda
- 1/4 teaspoon baking powder
- 1/4 teaspoon salt
- 1 1/2 sticks plus 3 tablespoons unsalted butter, softened
- 1 1/2 cups granulated sugar
- 2 large eggs, at room temperature

- 1 teaspoon pure vanilla extract
- 1 cup creamy peanut butter
- 2/3 cup confectioners' sugar
- 1 cup heavy cream
- 8 ounces semisweet chocolate, chopped

Direction

- Preheat the oven to 350° and position 2 racks in the lower and middle third of the oven.
- Line 24 muffin cups with paper or foil liners.
- Put the cocoa powder in a medium heatproof bowl.
- Add the boiling water and whisk until a smooth paste forms.
- Whisk in the buttermilk until combined.
- In a medium bowl, sift the flour with the baking soda, baking powder and salt.
- In a large bowl, using an electric mixer, beat 1 1/2 sticks of the butter with the granulated sugar until light and fluffy, about 3 minutes.
- Beat in the eggs and vanilla, then beat in the dry ingredients in 2 batches, alternating with the cocoa mixture.
- Carefully spoon the cupcake batter into the lined muffin cups, filling them about two-thirds full.
- Bake for 20 to 22 minutes, or until the cupcakes are springy.
- Let the cupcakes cool in the pans for 5 minutes, then transfer them to wire racks to cool completely.
- In a medium bowl, beat the peanut butter with the remaining 3 tablespoons of butter until creamy.
- Sift the confectioners' sugar into the bowl and beat until light and fluffy, about 2 minutes.
- Spoon all but 3 tablespoons of the peanut butter filling into a pastry bag fitted with a 1/4-inch star tip.
- Holding a cupcake in your hand, plunge the tip into the top of the cake, pushing it about 3/4 inch deep.
- Gently squeeze the pastry bag to fill the cupcake, withdrawing it slowly as you squeeze; you will feel the cupcake expand slightly as you fill it.
- Scrape any filling from the top of the cupcake and repeat until all of the cupcakes are filled.
- In a small saucepan, bring the heavy cream to a simmer.
- Off the heat, add the semisweet chocolate to the cream and let stand for 5 minutes, then whisk the melted chocolate into the cream until smooth.
- Let the chocolate icing stand until slightly cooled and thickened, about 15 minutes.
- Dip the tops of the cupcakes into the icing, letting the excess drip back into the pan.
- Transfer the cupcakes to racks and let stand for 5 minutes.
- Dip the tops of the cupcakes again and transfer them to racks. Spoon the remaining 3 tablespoons of peanut butter filling into the pastry bag and pipe tiny rosettes on the tops of the cupcakes.
- MAKE AHEAD the cupcakes are best served the same day they are made, but they can be refrigerated overnight in an airtight container.
- Tip:
- If you don't have a pastry bag with a fitted tip, you can fill these cupcakes by carving a hole in the centre (from the top) with a sharp paring knife. Put the filling in a resealable plastic bag and snip off one of the corners. Pipe the filling directly into the hole.

76. Devils Food Cake With Brown Sugar Buttercream Recipe

Serving: 24 | Prep: | Cook: 60mins | Ready in:

Ingredients

- Devil's Food Cake:
- 1 c. boiling water
- 3/4 c. unsweetened cocoa powder (not Dutch-process)
- 1/2 c. whole milk
- 1 tsp. vanilla
- 2 c. all-purpose flour

- 1 1/4 tsp. baking soda
- 1/2 tsp. salt
- 2 sticks (1 c.) unsalted butter, softened
- 1 1/4 c. packed dark brown sugar
- 3/4 c. granulated sugar
- 4 large eggs
- brown sugar Buttercream:
- 3 large egg whites at room temperature
- 3/4 tsp. salt
- 1 c. packed dark brown sugar
- 1/2 c. water
- 1/2 tsp. fresh lemon juice
- 3 sticks (1 1/2 c.) unsalted butter, cut into pieces and softened
- 2 tsp. vanilla

Direction

- For cake:
- Preheat oven to 350 F. Butter three 8 X 2-in. round cake pans and line bottoms of each with rounds of wax or parchment paper. Butter paper and dust pans with flour, knocking out excess.
- Whisk together boiling water and cocoa powder in a bowl until smooth, then whisk in milk and vanilla. Sift together flour, baking soda, and salt in another bowl.
- Beat together butter and sugars in a large bowl with an electric mixer until pale and fluffy, then add eggs 1 at a time, beating well after each addition. Beat in flour and cocoa mixtures alternately in batches, beginning and ending with flour mixture (batter may look curdled).
- Divide batter among pans, smoothing tops. Bake in upper and lower thirds of oven, switching position of pans halfway through baking, until a tester comes out clean and layers begin to pull away from sides of pans, 20 to 25 minutes total. Cool layers in pans on racks 10 minutes, then invert onto racks, remove wax paper, and cool completely.
- Buttercream:
- Combine egg whites and salt in a large bowl.
- Stir together brown sugar and water in a small heavy saucepan and bring to a boil over moderately high heat, washing down side of pan with a pastry brush dipped in water.
- When sugar syrup reaches boil, start beating whites with an electric mixer at medium-high speed until frothy, then add lemon juice and beat at medium speed until whites just hold soft peaks. (Do not beat again until sugar syrup is ready.)
- Meanwhile, put candy thermometer into sugar syrup and continue boiling until syrup reaches 238–242 F. Immediately remove from heat and pour into a heatproof 1-cup glass measure. Slowly pour hot syrup in a thin stream down side of bowl into egg whites, beating constantly at high speed. Beat meringue, scraping down bowl with a rubber spatula, until meringue is cool to the touch, about 6 minutes. (It's important that meringue is properly cooled before proceeding.)
- With mixer at medium speed, gradually add butter 1 piece at a time, beating well after each addition until incorporated. (If meringue is too warm and buttercream looks soupy after some of butter is added, briefly chill bottom of bowl in a large bowl filled with ice water for a few seconds before continuing to beat in remaining butter.) Continue beating until buttercream is smooth. (Mixture may look curdled before all of butter is added, but will come back together before beating is finished.) Add vanilla and beat 2 minutes more.
- To assemble:
- Put 1 cake layer, rounded side up, on a cake plate and spread with about 1 cup buttercream. Top with another cake layer, rounded side up, and spread with another cup buttercream. Top with remaining cake layer and frost top and sides of cake with remaining buttercream.

77. Devils Food Cupcakes With Marshmallow Filling Recipe

Serving: 16 | Prep: | Cook: 20mins | Ready in:

Ingredients

- 3/4 cup (3/8 lb.) butter, at room temperature
- 1 1/2 cups sugar
- 2 large eggs
- 2 cups all-purpose flour
- 1/2 cup Dutch-process unsweetened cocoa
- 2 teaspoons baking powder
- 1/2 teaspoon salt
- 1 cup milk
- 1 jar (7 oz.) marshmallow cream
- chocolate cream cheese frosting

Direction

- 1. In a bowl, with a mixer on medium speed, beat butter and sugar until smooth. Add eggs, one at a time, beating well after each addition and scraping down sides of bowl as needed.
- 2. In another bowl, mix flour, cocoa, baking powder, and salt. Stir in half the flour mixture into butter mixture. Stir in milk just until blended. Add remaining flour mixture and stir just until incorporated. Spoon batter equally into 16 muffin cups (1/3-cup capacity; cups should be almost full) lined with paper baking cups.
- 3. Bake in a 350° regular or convection oven until tops spring back when lightly pressed in the centre or a wooden skewer inserted into the centre comes out clean, about 20 minutes. Let cool in pans on racks for 5 minutes; remove cupcakes from pans and set on racks to cool completely, at least 30 minutes.
- 4. With a small, sharp knife, cut a cylinder about 3/4 inch wide and 1 inch deep from the centre of the top of each cupcake. Trim off and discard about 1/2 inch from bottom of each cylinder. With a knife, hollow out a small cavity inside each cupcake.
- 5. Spoon marshmallow cream into pastry bag fitted with a 1/2-inch plain tip. Twist end of bag tightly to secure. Place tip in cavity of one cupcake; without moving tip, squeeze filling into cavity, to 1/4 inch from top. Repeat to fill remaining cupcakes. Insert cake cylinders into holes.
- 6. Spoon chocolate cream cheese frosting into another pastry bag, fitted with a 3/4-inch star tip, and pipe onto tops of cupcakes, or spread on cupcakes with knife.

78. Diabetic Low Fat Orange Muffins Eggless Recipe

Serving: 12 | Prep: | Cook: 25mins | Ready in:

Ingredients

- vegetable cooking spray
- 2 cups unbleached flour
- 1 Tbls baking powder
- 1/4 cup sugar
- 6 oz orange juice, frozen concentrate, thawed
- 2 Tbls canola oil
- 1 Tbls nonfat plain yogurt
- 1/2 cup apricot preserves, low sugar
- 2 Tbls dried apples, chopped
- 1 Tbls sugar
- 1/4 tsp cinnamon
- 1/4 tsp ground nutmeg
- Topping:
- 1 Tbls sugar
- 1/4 tsp cinnamon
- 1/4 tsp ground nutmeg

Direction

- Preheat oven to 375F. Spray 12 muffin tins with cooking spray.
- Mix the flour, baking powder, and 1/4 cup sugar together. Set aside.
- In a large bowl, beat the thoroughly thawed orange juice concentrate, oil, yogurt, and apricot preserves together.
- Stir in the apricots.
- Slowly stir the flour mixture into the liquid ingredients just until everything is moistened. Do not overmix.
- Spoon the batter into the muffin tins.

- Mix the sugar, cinnamon, and nutmeg together, and sprinkle over the muffins.
- Bake for 20 to 25 minutes or until a cake tester comes out clean.
- Makes 1 dozen.

79. Double Dark Chocolate Sesame Cakes Recipe

Serving: 24 | Prep: | Cook: 25mins | Ready in:

Ingredients

- 1 cup flour
- 1 cup whole wheat flour
- 3/4 cup unsweetened cocoa powder
- 1 cup sugar
- 2 tsp baking soda
- 1 tsp baking powder
- 1/2 tsp salt
- 5 oz low-fat silken tofu, pureed
- 1 cup cooled, strong coffee
- 1 cup fat free soymilk
- 1 tbsp lemon juice
- 1/2 cup toasted sesame seed oil
- 3 tbsp black sesame seeds, toasted

Direction

- Preheat oven to 375F.
- In a large bowl, whisk together the flours, cocoa powder, sugar, baking soda, baking powder and salt.
- Make a well in the center and pour in the tofu, coffee, soymilk, lemon juice and oil.
- Stir until smooth, then mix in the sesame seeds.
- Spoon the batter into prepared cups, dividing evenly.
- Bake 25 minutes. Cool in the pan set over a wire rack for 20 minutes, then unmould and cool completely.

80. Double Chocolate Marble Cupcakes Recipe

Serving: 26 | Prep: | Cook: 25mins | Ready in:

Ingredients

- milk chocolate Batter
- 190 g granulated sugar
- 87 g flour
- 35 g unsweetened cocoa
- 25 g powdered skim milk powder
- 3 g baking powder
- 3 g baking soda
- pinch salt
- 1 egg
- 250 mL whole milk
- 60 mL canola oil
- 10 mL vanilla
- ---
- dark chocolate Batter
- 87g flour
- 45g unsweetened cocoa (dark if you can get it)
- 3 g baking powder
- 3 g baking soda
- pinch salt
- 1 egg
- 250 mL brewed, cooled coffee
- 60 mL canola oil
- 5 mL vanilla
- 150 g dark brown sugar

Direction

- Preheat oven to 350F, grease or line muffin cups.
- In a bowl, whisk together granulated sugar, flour, cocoa, milk powder, baking powder, baking soda and salt. Set aside.
- Beat together egg, milk, oil and vanilla, set aside.
- In another bowl, combine the second amounts of flour, cocoa, baking powder, baking soda and salt.
- Separately, beat together the second egg, coffee, oil, vanilla and brown sugar.

- Add the milk mixture to the first bowl of dry ingredients and beat 2 minutes.
- Add the coffee mixture to the second bowl of dry ingredients and beat 2 minutes.
- Dollop amounts of milk and dark chocolate batters into the prepared cups, filling no more than 2/3 of the way full.
- Use a chopstick or skewer to lightly swirl the batters.
- Bake 23-25 minutes, until the toothpick test comes clean. Cool in tins 10 minutes before turning out onto rack and cooling completely.

81. Easter Basket Cupcakes Recipe

Serving: 32 | Prep: | Cook: 25mins | Ready in:

Ingredients

- Cupcake Batter:
- 3 C. flour
- 2 C. granulated sugar
- 2 tsp. baking soda
- 2 tsp. salt
- 2/3 C. cocoa powder
- 1 C. vegetable oil
- 2 C. water
- 2 tsp. vanilla extract
- 2 tbsp. white vinegar
- Frosting:
- 1 C. butter, softened
- 3 1/2 C. confectioners sugar
- 1 tsp. milk
- 1 tsp. vanilla extract
- 1/8 tsp. salt
- green food coloring (or other desired color), as needed
- Decorating:
- 1 pkg. Candy eggs (Whopper eggs work well)
- 32 chocolate Twizzlers (for handles)
- Shredded dry coconut, colored as desired with food coloring (optional)
- jelly beans, marshmallow Peeps, and other candies (optional)

Direction

- 1. Preheat oven to 350 degrees F.
- 2. In a large mixing bowl, combine dry ingredients with a fork. Add oil, water, vanilla, and vinegar. Blend well.
- 3. Divide mixture evenly between prepared, paper-lined cupcake tins (about 32).
- 4. Bake 20-25 minutes, or until toothpick inserted in the centre comes out clean.
- 5. Let cool completely on wire racks before frosting and decorating.
- Instructions for frosting:
- 1. In a medium mixing bowl, beat butter until fluffy. Add powdered sugar and salt. Blend well.
- 2. Add milk and vanilla. Beat several minutes over medium-high speed until smooth and fluffy.
- Instructions for decorating:
- Frost and decorate as desired with colored coconut (learn how to do this here), jelly beans or chocolate eggs. When frosted and decorated, insert each end of one Twizzlers (chocolate looks best, but you can use any flavour) firmly into the cupcake to make a basket. This is one of the best Easter dessert recipes to make with the kids

82. Easy Pumpkin Cupcakes Recipe

Serving: 24 | Prep: | Cook: 60mins | Ready in:

Ingredients

- 1-15 oz can of pumpkin
- 3 eggs
- 1/2 cup veg. oil
- 1 tsp. baking soda
- 2 tsp. cinnamon or pumpkin pie spice
- 1 pkg. yellow cake mix
- cream cheese frosting

Direction

- Mix together: pumpkin, eggs, oil, baking soda, and spice.
- Add the cake mix.
- Beat for 1 min. on low.
- Beat an addition 2 min. on high.
- Fill cupcake liners 3/4 full.
- Bake at 350 for 20 min. or until toothpick comes out clean.
- Cool
- Frost with frosting of choice (cream cheese is our favourite)

83. Easy Red Velvet Cupcakes Recipe

Serving: 24 | Prep: | Cook: 55mins |Ready in:

Ingredients

- 1 pkg. (2 layer size) red velvet cake mix
- 1 pkg. (3.9 oz) chocolate instant pudding
- 1 pkg (8oz) cream cheese,softened
- 1/2 c butter,softened
- 1 pkg (16 oz) powdered sugar (4 c)
- 1 c thawed whipped topping
- 1 square whie chocolate,shaved into curls

Direction

- Prepare cake batter and bake as directed on pkg. for cupcakes, blending dry pudding mix into batter before spooning into prepared muffin cups. Cool.
- Meanwhile, beat cream cheese and butter in large bowl with mixer until well blended. Gradually beat in sugar. Whisk in whipped topping. Spoon 1-1/2 c into small freezer-weight resealable bag; seal bag. Cut small corner off bottom of bag. Insert tip of bag into top of each cupcake to pipe about 1 Tbsp. frosting into the centre of each.
- Frost cupcakes with remaining frosting. Top with chocolate curls. Keep refrigerated.

84. Egg Free Chocolate Cupcakes Recipe

Serving: 12 | Prep: | Cook: 30mins |Ready in:

Ingredients

- Cupcakes:
- 1 1/2 c. all-purpose flour
- 1 c. sugar
- 1/4 c. baking cocoa
- 1 tsp. baking soda
- 1/2 tsp. salt
- 1 c. water
- 1/3 c. vegetable oil
- 1 Tbs. white vinegar
- 1 tsp. vanilla
- Icing:
- 6 tablespoons butter, softened
- 3 tablespoons milk or soymilk
- 1 teaspoon vanilla
- 3 cups confectioners' sugar
- food coloring (optional)

Direction

- For cupcakes: Combine flour, sugar, cocoa, baking soda, and salt. Add water, oil, vinegar, and vanilla. Mix well. Fill paper-lined muffin cups 3/4 full with batter. Bake at 350ºF for 25-30 minutes. Cool 10 minutes and remove from pan. Makes 12.
- For icing: In a bowl, beat together the butter, milk/soymilk and vanilla until smooth (about 3 minutes). Add in confectioners' sugar; beat very well until smooth, adding more if necessary to achieve desired consistency. Add in food colouring (if desired) and mix well.

85. Eileens Cream Cheese Chocolate Cupcakes Recipe

Serving: 18 | Prep: | Cook: 35mins | Ready in:

Ingredients

- Filling
- 1 (8-oz) carton cream cheese, softened
- 1/3-cup sugar
- 1 egg
- 1/8-tspn salt
- 1-cup semi-sweet chocolate pieces
- 1-cup peanut butter chips
- Cupcakes
- 1 ½-cups flour
- 1-cup sugar
- 1/4-cup baking cocoa
- 1/4-tspn baking soda
- 1/2-tspn salt
- 1-cup water
- 1/2-cup vegetable oil
- 1-tbspn white vinegar
- 1-tspn vanilla extract

Direction

- For the filling-
- In a bowl, beat the cream cheese until smooth.
- Add the sugar, egg, add salt, mix well.
- Foil in the chocolate and peanut butter chips set aside.
- For the cupcakes -
- In a bowl, combine the flour, sugar, cocoa, baking soda, and salt Add the water, oil, vinegar, and vanilla; mix well.
- Fill paper-lined muffin cups half full with batter.
- Top each with about 2-tbspn of cream cheese filling.
- Bake at 350 degrees for 30 - 35 minutes.
- Cook for 10 minutes before removing to write rack to
- Cool completely.
- Yields 1 ½-dz.
- NOTE: The filling with partially cover the top of the cupcake.

- -Susana

86. Elaines Triple Chocolate Muffins Recipe

Serving: 6 | Prep: | Cook: 25mins | Ready in:

Ingredients

- 1 ½ cups cake & pastry flour
- 1 tsp baking soda
- 1 1/14 tsp baking powder
- ¼ tsp salt
- 3 whole eggs
- 1 cup water
- ½ cup olive oil
- 1 tsp vanilla extract
- 4 tbsp dark, unsweetened cocoa
- 4 tbsp raw sugar
- ¾ cup white chocolate bits
- For the Icing:
- 1 ½ cups confectioners' sugar
- 1 tsp cream of tartar
- 1 beaten egg
- 3 tbsp dark, unsweetened cocoa

Direction

- Assemble all dry ingredients for both cupcakes and icing in separate bowls.
- Add wet ingredients to both as indicated in each section.
- Chill the icing until ready to use.
- Spoon cupcake mixture into cups, filling ¾ full.
- On top of each cup of batter, sprinkle a generous amount of white chocolate chips or bits.
- Bake cupcakes in ungreased pan in cupcake liners, at 375*F for 25 to 30 minutes, or until muffins spring back in the center when touched.
- Allow muffins to cool in the pan before icing them.

- Ice generously, then top each muffin with a few white chocolate chips to decorate.

87. Elvis Cupcakes Recipe

Serving: 18 | Prep: | Cook: 20mins | Ready in:

Ingredients

- 2 cups all purpose flour
- 3/4 cup sugar
- 1 tsp. baking soda
- 1/2 tsp. salt
- 1 cup mayonnaise
- 1-1/3 cups mashed ripe bananas (about 3 medium)
- 1 tsp. vanilla extract
- 18 milk chocolate kisses
- peanut butter Frosting:
- 1/3 cup creamy peanut butter
- 2 cups powdered sugar
- 1 tsp. vanilla extract
- 3 to 4 Tblsp. milk
- milk chocolate chips, optional

Direction

- Cupcakes:
- In a large bowl, combine the flour, sugar, baking soda and salt.
- In another bowl, combine the mayonnaise, bananas, and vanilla;
- Stir into dry ingredients just until combined.
- Spoon 1 Tbsp. batter into each paper-lined muffin cup.
- Top each with a chocolate kiss, pointed side down.
- Fill cups two-thirds full with remaining batter.
- Bake at 350 for 20-25 minutes or until toothpick tests done.
- Cool for 10 min. before removing from pans to wire racks to cool completely.
- Frosting:
- In a large bowl, combine the peanut butter, confectioner's sugar, vanilla and enough milk to achieve spreading consistency.
- Frost cupcakes.
- Garnish with chocolate chips, if desired.

88. Espresso Cupcakes With Milk Chocolate Ganache And White Chocolate Frosting Recipe

Serving: 68 | Prep: | Cook: 20mins | Ready in:

Ingredients

- Makes 12 cupcakes
- CUPCAKES:
- 1/2 teaspoon baking soda
- 1/2 teaspoon baking powder
- 1/4 teaspoon salt
- 2 teaspoons instant espresso powder
- 4 ounces (8 tablespoons) unsalted butter, softened
- 1 cup granulated sugar
- 2 large eggs
- 1/2 cup milk
- milk chocolate GANACHE:
- 2/3 cup heavy (whipping) cream
- 5 1/2 ounces milk chocolate, finely chopped
- white chocolate FROSTING:
- 4 1/2 ounces white chocolate. finely chopped
- 1 3/4 cups confectioners' sugar
- 1/4 cup milk
- 1/2 teaspoon vanilla extract
- 3 ounces (6 tablespoons) unsalted butter, softened
- Pinch of salt

Direction

- TO MAKE THE CUPCAKES: Preheat the oven to 350 degrees F. Line 12 cupcake wells with paper liners.
- Sift together the flour, baking soda, baking powder, and salt. Stir in the espresso powder.

- Using an electric mixer on medium speed, beat the butter with the granulated sugar until light, 1 minute with a stand mixer or 2 minutes with a handheld mixer. Add the eggs, one at a time, beating well after each addition. Continue to beat the mixture for 1 minute with a stand mixer or 2 minutes with a handheld mixer.
- On low speed, alternately add the dry ingredients and the milk in 2 additions, stirring until incorporated after each addition.
- Pour the batter into the paper-lined cupcake wells. Bake until a skewer inserted in the middle comes out clean, about 20 minutes. Let cool to room temperature, then remove from the pans.
- TO MAKE THE GANACHE: Place the cream in a small, heavy-bottomed saucepan and warm over medium-high heat until it begins to bubble around the edges, about 5 minutes. Remove the pan from the stove, add the chocolate, and whisk until smooth. Transfer to a bowl and place plastic wrap directly over the ganache. Refrigerate until cold.
- TO MAKE THE FROSTING: Melt the white chocolate in a double boiler. Stir until smooth. Let cool to room temperature.
- Sift the confectioners' sugar into a medium bowl. Stir in the milk and vanilla. Add the butter and salt and beat until smooth. Stir in the cooled white chocolate. Refrigerate until firm enough to frost the cupcakes, about 30 minutes.
- Cut out about one quarter of the inside of each cupcake with a small paring knife. Fill the indent with the milk chocolate ganache. Frost each cupcake with the white chocolate frosting.

89. Fairy Cakes Recipe

Serving: 12 | Prep: | Cook: 20mins | Ready in:

Ingredients

- 1/2 cup unsalted butter, softened
- 7 Tablespoons sugar
- 2 large eggs
- 3/4 cup self-rising cake flour
- 1 teaspoon pure vanilla extract
- Note: I have used 1/2 teaspoon almond extract instead of the suggested 1 tsp. vanilla extract and the flavour is amazing.
- 2-3 Tablespoons milk
- This is your typical hard Icing:
- Note: I do not like this icing recipe because it dries out too quickly and believe me, when I say dries it hardens and dries. Not my suggestion. I prefer a butter cream icing for these dainties.
- 1 cup powdered sugar
- 1 egg white
- 3-4 drops lemon juice
- food coloring

Direction

- Preheat oven to 400 degrees F.
- Line a 12 cup muffin tin with baking cups.
- Put all the ingredients except for the milk into a food processor and blend until smooth.
- Pulse while adding the milk down the funnel to make for a soft consistency.
- It doesn't seem like enough, but you can get enough into each baking cup, just scrape it all out and try to fill each one equally.
- Bake for 15-20 minutes or until they are golden on top.
- Cool on a wire rack, but remove from the tin as soon as possible.
- Before you decorate, slice off any mounded tops so you have a flat surface to decorate.
- Icing:
- Mix the sugar, egg white and lemon juice in a small bowl until smooth and creamy, it should have the consistency of heavy cream Nigella always breaks the batch into smaller batches so she can have different colours.

90. Favorite Chocolate Cupcakes Recipe

Serving: 24 | Prep: | Cook: 30mins | Ready in:

Ingredients

- 2 cups White Lily® all-purpose flour
- 2 cups sugar
- 3/4 cup unsweetened cocoa powder
- 1 teaspoon baking soda
- 1 teaspoon salt
- 1/2 cup butter, melted
- 1/4 cup Crisco® oil
- 1/2 cup buttermilk
- 2 eggs
- 2 teaspoons vanilla
- 1 cup boiling water
- chocolate frosting
- 1/2 cup butter, softened
- 1/2 cup unsweetened cocoa powder
- 3 cups sifted confectioners' sugar
- 3-4 tablespoons milk
- 1 teaspoon vanilla

Direction

- Preheat oven to 350°F.
- Line 24 muffin cups with paper or foil liners.
- In large bowl, whisk together flour, sugar, cocoa, soda and salt. Add butter, oil, buttermilk, eggs and vanilla. Beat two minutes at medium speed.
- Stir in water until blended. Batter will be thin.
- Divide batter among muffin cups. Bake at 350°F for 30-35 min, or until toothpick inserted near centre comes out clean.
- Cool in pan 5 min. Remove to wire rack. Cool completely.
- Frosting:
- In large mixing bowl, beat butter and cocoa until creamy. Add sugar, 3 tablespoons milk and vanilla. Beat on low until blended. Beat on medium until light and fluffy. Add more milk if frosting is too thick. Makes enough to frost 24 cupcakes.

91. Frog Cupcakes

Serving: 0 | Prep: | Cook: | Ready in:

Ingredients

- 1 (18.25 ounce) package white cake mix
- 1 (16 ounce) can prepared vanilla frosting
- 6 drops green food coloring, or as needed
- ¼ cup green decorator sugar
- 12 regulars large marshmallows
- 48 eaches semisweet chocolate chips
- 1 drop red food coloring

Direction

- Bake cupcakes according to the directions on the package. Allow them to cool completely.
- Scoop 2/3 of the frosting into a small bowl and mix with green food coloring. Frost the cupcakes. Sprinkle some of the green sugar over the tops.
- Cut the marshmallows in half to make two circles. Dip half of each marshmallow piece into water and dip into the green sugar to make the eyelids. The remaining white will be the eyes. Place on the cupcakes. Use a little bit of white icing to glue a chocolate chip into the center of each eye for the pupil.
- Mix the remaining frosting with red food coloring to make pink. Use the pink icing to draw smiling mouths and nostrils or even tongues on the frogs.
- Nutrition Facts
- Per Serving:
- 341.5 calories; protein 2.4g 5% DV; carbohydrates 54.5g 18% DV; fat 15g 23% DV; cholesterolmg; sodium 182.1mg 7% DV.

92. Graveyard Cupcakes Recipe

Serving: 18 | Prep: | Cook: 22mins | Ready in:

Ingredients

- Cake:
- 1 1/2 cups flour
- 1/2 cup cocoa powder
- 3/4 teaspoon baking soda
- 1/4 teaspoon salt
- 1/2 cup butter, room temperature
- 1 1/3 cups sugar
- 1 teaspoon vanilla
- 2 large eggs
- 1 cup milk
- Frosting:
- 1/4 cup butter, room temperature
- 4 cups confectioner's sugar
- 1/3 cup milk
- 1 teaspoon vanilla
- 3 ounces unsweetened chocolate, melted
- Topping:
- chocolate chessmen cookies (or wafer cookies)
- Candy pumpkins (I use jelly Belly)
- Deluxe Grahams chocolate covered graham crackers
- icing writer

Direction

- Cakes:
- Preheat oven to 350.
- Whisk flour, cocoa, baking soda, and salt together in small bowl; set aside.
- In large bowl, beat butter until creamy. Add sugar gradually, beating until light and fluffy. Beat in vanilla. Beat in eggs, one at a time. Add flour mixture alternately with milk. Beat until smooth.
- Divide batter among cupcake pan with liners.
- Bake 22 minutes.
- Cool in pans for 5 minutes, then remove to cool completely.
- Frosting:
- In a large bowl, beat butter until creamy. Add 1 cup of sugar gradually, beating until light and fluffy. Add remaining 3 cups of sugar and the milk. Beat until smooth and creamy. Add vanilla and chocolate. Beat until combined.
- Assembly:
- Use icing writer to decorate chocolate covered grahams with RIPs and crosses.
- Crush chocolate cookies in a large Ziploc bag until they are the consistency of dirt.
- Frost cupcakes then hold each one over a bowl of the "dirt" and sprinkle generously.
- Insert tombstone.
- Place pumpkin.

93. Heavenly Cupcakes Recipe

Serving: 12 | Prep: | Cook: 25mins | Ready in:

Ingredients

- CUP cakeS
- 125 g. unsweetened chocolate, chopped
- 6 tablespoon unsalted butter, at room temperature
- 3 extra - large whole eggs, lightly beaten, plus 3 extra large egg whites
- 1/2 cup granulated sugar
- 2 tablespoon all purpose flour
- FOR THE chocolate whipped cream
- 2 cups heavy cream chilled
- 1 cup confectioner's sugar, sifted.
- 1/2 cup unsweetened cocoa, sifted before measuring.

Direction

- Preheat oven to 350 F. 9180.C). Line 12 muffin pan cups with fluted paper cups.
- Bring a saucepan one-fourth full of water to a gentle simmer.
- Place the chocolate and butter in a large, heatproof bowl over (not touching) the water, stir until melted and smooth. Let cool for 5 minutes. Stir in the whole eggs, granulated sugar, and flour.
- Meanwhile, place the egg whites in a separated bowl. using an electric mixer set on high speed, beat until stiff and glossy but not dry, Using a rubber spatula, fold the egg whites into the chocolate mixture. Spoon into

the muffin cups, filling each cup only two-thirds full.
- Bake until the top looks dry and a toothpick inserted into the centre of a cupcake comes out clean, 12 - 14 minutes. Transfer to a wire rack to cool before icing.
- TO MAKE THE WHIPPED CREAM...
- Using a chilled metal bowl and chilled beaters, whip the cream for a few minutes until it starts to thicken. Add the sifted confectioner's sugar and sifted cocoa and continue beating until thick enough to hold firm peaks. Take care to not overbeat or the cream will turn butter.
- Top each cupcake with some of the chocolate whipped cream. Serve. If refrigerating before serving, chill for no more than 6 hours.

94. Hi Hat Cupcakes Recipe

Serving: 12 | Prep: | Cook: 20mins | Ready in:

Ingredients

- Makes 12 cupcakes
- FOR THE BATTER
- 3 ounces unsweetened chocolate, chopped
- 1 cup all-purpose flour
- 1/2 teaspoon baking powder
- 1/2 teaspoon baking soda
- 1/4 teaspoon salt
- 1/2 cup (1 stick) unsalted butter, softened
- 1 1/4 cups sugar
- 2 large eggs
- 1 teaspoon vanilla extract
- 1/2 cup sour cream
- FOR THE frosting
- 1 3/4 cups sugar
- 3 large egg whites
- 1/4 teaspoon cream of tartar
- 1 teaspoon vanilla extract
- 1/2 teaspoon almond extract
- FOR THE chocolate COATING
- 2 cups chopped (about 12 ounces) semisweet chocolate
- 3 tablespoons canola or vegetable oil

Direction

- Directions
- Preheat oven to 350 degrees with rack in centre. Prepare the batter: Place chocolate in a medium heatproof bowl, and set it over a medium saucepan of barely simmering water; stir chocolate until melted and smooth. Remove bowl from heat, and set aside to cool slightly.
- Meanwhile, whisk together flour, baking powder, baking soda, and salt in a medium bowl; set aside.
- In the bowl of an electric mixer fitted with the paddle attachment, cream butter and sugar on medium speed, scraping sides of bowl as needed, until light and fluffy. On low speed, mix in melted chocolate. Increase speed to medium, and add eggs, one at a time, mixing well after each addition. Add vanilla, and beat until mixture is creamy and colour has lightened slightly, about 1 minute. Mix in sour cream. On low speed, add half of reserved flour mixture, beating until just incorporated. Mix in 1/2 cup water. Add remaining flour mixture, and mix until just incorporated.
- Line a cupcake pan with paper liners. Fill each liner with enough batter to come 1/8 inch from top, about 1/3 cup. Bake, rotating pans halfway through, until tops are firm and a cake tester inserted in the centre comes out clean, about 20 minutes. Transfer cupcakes to a wire rack to cool in pan for 10 minutes.
- Use a small knife to loosen any tops stuck to the pan. Carefully invert cupcakes onto the wire rack. Turn cupcakes right side up, and let cool completely.
- Prepare the frosting: In a large heatproof bowl, combine sugar, 1/4 cup water, egg whites, and cream of tartar. Using a handheld electric mixer, beat on high speed until foamy, about 1 minute. Set bowl over a pan of barely simmering water. Beat on high speed until frosting forms stiff peaks, about 12 minutes; frosting should register 160 degrees on a

candy thermometer. Remove from heat; stir in vanilla and almond extracts, and beat for 2 minutes more until frosting thickens.

- Transfer frosting to a large pastry bag fitted with a 1/2-inch plain pastry tip. Leaving a 1/8-inch border on each cupcake, pipe a spiral of frosting into a 2-inch-high cone shape, using about 1/2 cup of frosting per cupcake. Transfer cupcakes to a baking sheet, and refrigerate while preparing the chocolate coating.
- Prepare the chocolate coating: Combine chocolate and oil in a medium heat-proof bowl set over a medium saucepan of barely simmering water; stir until melted and smooth. Transfer to a small bowl, and let cool about 15 minutes.
- Holding each cupcake by its bottom, dip cupcake in the chocolate to coat frosting, allowing excess to drip off. Transfer to a baking sheet fitted with a wire rack. Spoon more coating around edge of cupcake and any exposed frosting; none of the frosting should show. Let cupcakes stand at room temperature 15 minutes.
- Carefully remove paper liners from cupcakes, and discard. Place cupcakes on a serving platter, and refrigerate for 30 minutes to let coating set. Cover, and refrigerate for 2 hours more. Serve cold. Cupcakes can be refrigerated for up to 3 days.

95. Hi Hat Cupcakes Recipe

Serving: 12 | Prep: | Cook: 20mins | Ready in:

Ingredients

- FOR THE BATTER
- ----------------------------
- 3 ounces unsweetened chocolate, chopped
- 1 cup all-purpose flour
- 1/2 teaspoon baking powder
- 1/2 teaspoon baking soda
- 1/4 teaspoon salt
- 1/2 cup (1 stick) unsalted butter, softened
- 1 1/4 cups sugar
- 2 large eggs
- 1 teaspoon vanilla extract
- 1/2 cup sour cream
- FOR THE frosting
- ----------------------------
- 1 3/4 cups sugar
- 3 large egg whites
- 1/4 teaspoon cream of tartar
- 1 teaspoon vanilla extract
- 1/2 teaspoon almond extract
- FOR THE chocolate COATING
- ----------------------------
- 2 cups chopped (about 12 ounces) semisweet chocolate
- 3 tablespoons canola or vegetable oil

Direction

- Preheat oven to 350 degrees with rack in centre.
- Prepare the batter: Place chocolate in a medium heatproof bowl, and set it over a medium saucepan of barely simmering water; stir chocolate until melted and smooth.
- Remove bowl from heat, and set aside to cool slightly.
- Meanwhile, whisk together flour, baking powder, baking soda, and salt in a medium bowl; set aside.
- In the bowl of an electric mixer fitted with the paddle attachment, cream butter and sugar on medium speed, scraping sides of bowl as needed, until light and fluffy.
- On low speed, mix in melted chocolate. Increase speed to medium, and add eggs, one at a time, mixing well after each addition. Add vanilla, and beat until mixture is creamy and colour has lightened slightly, about 1 minute.
- Mix in sour cream.
- On low speed, add half of reserved flour mixture, beating until just incorporated.
- Mix in 1/2 cup water. Add remaining flour mixture, and mix until just incorporated.

- Line a cupcake pan with paper liners. Fill each liner with enough batter to come 1/8 inch from top, about 1/3 cup.
- Bake, rotating pans halfway through, until tops are firm and a cake tester inserted in the centre comes out clean, about 20 minutes.
- Transfer cupcakes to a wire rack to cool in pan for 10 minutes.
- Use a small knife to loosen any tops stuck to the pan. Carefully invert cupcakes onto the wire rack. Turn cupcakes right side up, and let cool completely.
- Prepare the frosting:

96. Ho Ho Cupcakes Recipe

Serving: 24 | Prep: | Cook: 28mins | Ready in:

Ingredients

- Cake:
- *If you're really in a hurry, use a boxed cake mix instead of this homemade one.
- ½ cup butter
- 1 cup water
- ½ cup any cooking oil (I've never tried olive oil)
- 4 tablespoons cocoa
- 2 eggs, beaten
- 2 cups sugar
- 2 cups flour
- 1 teaspoon baking soda
- ½ cup sour cream or buttermilk
- Filling:
- 1 cup sugar
- ½ cup half-and-half or whole milk
- 1 teaspoon vanilla extract
- 1 cup solid shortening (regular, not the buttery flavored, and you really can't substitute butter for the shortening…it doesn't give the same end result)
- 1 tablespoon water
- ¼ teaspoon salt
- 1½ to 2 cups powdered sugar (enough to make filling thick enough)
- Frosting:
- 1 cup sugar
- 6 tablespoons butter
- 6 tablespoons half-and-half or whole milk
- 1½ cups milk chocolate chips or semi-sweet chocolate chips, depending on your preference

Direction

- For the cake, mix butter, water, oil and cocoa in a medium saucepan.
- Cook until butter is melted, stirring constantly.
- Remove saucepan from heat.
- Add some of the cooked mixture to the beaten eggs to temper the eggs, then stir it into the saucepan mixture.
- Immediately beat in the sugar.
- Mix flour and baking soda together, adding the flour mixture to saucepan alternately with the sour cream, whisking ingredients together well.
- Line muffin tins with cupcake liners, and fill them 2/3 full of cake batter (I THINK it makes about 18 cupcakes, but it's been several years since I've made these, so I'm not absolutely certain about the quantity – have 24 tins ready, just in case I'm off!)
- Bake at 350 degrees for 18 to 24 minutes, until they test done.
- Remove pans from oven and take cupcakes out of tins to cool on wire racks.
- Allow cupcakes to cool completely before filling and frosting.
- While cupcakes are baking and cooling, prepare the filling and frosting.
- For the filling, beat sugar, half-and-half or milk, vanilla, solid shortening, water and salt for 5 minutes…the mixture should be very light and fluffy.
- Beat in enough powdered sugar until the filling is a consistency that is solid enough to hold its shape when scooped onto the cupcake, and won't run off of it.

- Prepare the frosting by placing the sugar, butter and milk into a medium saucepan and bringing it to a boil; boil for 1 minute.
- Remove pan from heat and stir in the chocolate chips, beating by hand until they are melted and frosting is thick and shiny.
- To assemble, have the same amount of CLEAN cupcake liners available to equal how many cupcakes you baked.
- Remove a cupcake from the cupcake liner it was baked in; cut the muffin in half lengthwise (side-to-side, not top to bottom).
- Place the bottom of the cupcake in a clean cupcake liner.
- Scoop a generous dollop of the filling over the cupcake bottom half.
- Frost the top half of the cupcake and place it on the filling.
- DONE…unless you're into decorating the tops of your cupcakes, but these really don't need anything else on them – they are quite rich enough!

97. Honey Cupcakes With Orange Icing Recipe

Serving: 12 | Prep: | Cook: 20mins | Ready in:

Ingredients

- Cupcakes:
- 1/2 c. whole wheat flour
- 1/2 c. all purpose flour
- 1/2 tsp. baking powder
- 1/4 tsp. baking soda
- 1/4 tsp. sea salt
- 1/3 c. skim milk
- 2 eggs
- 1/4 c. applesauce
- 1/4 c. olive oil
- 2/3 c. honey
- 1/2 tsp. vanilla
- Icing:
- 1 1/2 c. powdered sugar
- 1 1/2 T. orange juice
- 1/2 tsp. orange extract
- 1/2 tsp. orange zest

Direction

- Mix ingredients for icing. (You want to do this first, the longer it sits the thicker it gets)
- Mix all cupcake ingredients in a bowl until well blended.
- Pour into paper-lined muffin trays.
- Bake at 375 F for 20 min.
- Drizzle with icing.

98. Hot Chocolate And Grand Marnier Cupcakes Recipe

Serving: 12 | Prep: | Cook: 7mins | Ready in:

Ingredients

- 6 oz. bittersweet chocolate, chopped
- 2 tbls. butter, unsalted
- 1/2 cup sugar
- 2 large eggs
- 2 large egg yolks
- 2 tbls. Grand Marnier
- 1/4 cup AP flour
- whipped cream for topping

Direction

- Line 12 cup muffin tin with muffin papers
- In a saucepan, melt butter and chocolate until smooth
- Remove from heat
- Beat sugar, eggs, egg yolks, and Grand Marnier with hand mixer until thick ribbon falls when lifted from batter
- Sift flour
- Gently fold flour into batter folding over with rubber spatula
- Fold in chocolate mixture
- Cover and chill at least 1/2 hour (can be left in fridge as long as overnight)

- Preheat oven to 400
- Bake until tops are puffed and cracked, about 7 minutes
- Toothpick inserted into centre should come out with batter attached
- Top with whipped cream

99. Hot Cocoa Cupcakes Recipe

Serving: 12 | Prep: | Cook: 30mins | Ready in:

Ingredients

- Cake:
- 1 1/2 cups sugar
- 1 2/3 cups all-purpose flour
- 1/2 cup plus 1 tablespoon cocoa powder, preferably Dutch-processed
- 1/4 teaspoon baking powder
- 1/4 teaspoon baking soda
- 3/4 teaspoon salt
- 2 eggs
- 3/4 cup milk
- 1/3 cup plus 1 tablespoon vegetable oil
- 1/2 tablespoon pure vanilla extract
- 3/4 cups very hot water
- Topping:
- 1 cup heavy cream
- 1 tablespoon sugar or 1 can real whipped cream

Direction

- Make the Cake: Preheat the oven to 350 degrees F.
- Sift together the sugar, flour, cocoa, baking powder, baking soda, and salt. Transfer to a standing mixer fitted with a whisk attachment (or use a hand mixer) and blend briefly.
- Whisk together the eggs, milk, oil, and vanilla in a medium bowl. Add to the dry ingredients and mix at low speed for 5 minutes. Gradually add the hot water, mixing at low speed until just combined. The batter will be quite thin.
- Pour the batter into coffee cups and arrange them 1-inch apart on a sheet pan or a rectangular cake pan. Bake until a toothpick inserted in the centre comes out clean (a few crumbs are okay), and the centre feels firm to the touch, about 25 to 30 minutes. Let the cakes cool on the pan. (Don't remove the cakes from the cups!)
- Meanwhile, make the Topping: In a chilled bowl, combine the cream and sugar and whip, using a hand-mixer, until soft peaks form.
- When ready to serve, spoon the topping over the cakes to cover, so they look like a cups of cocoa topped with whipped cream. Serve with a spoon.

100. Ina Gartens Coconut Cupcakes Recipe

Serving: 60 | Prep: | Cook: 20mins | Ready in:

Ingredients

- 3/4 pound (3 sticks) unsalted butter, room temperature
- 2 cups sugar
- 5 extra-large eggs at room temperature
- 1 1/2 teaspoons pure vanilla extract
- 1 1/2 teaspoons pure almond extract
- 3 cups flour
- 1 teaspoon baking powder
- 1/2 teaspoon baking soda
- 1/2 teaspoon kosher salt
- 1 cup buttermilk
- 14 ounces sweetened, shredded coconut
- For the frosting:
- 1 pound cream cheese at room temperature
- 3/4 pound (3 sticks) unsalted butter, room temperature
- 1 teaspoon pure vanilla extract
- 1/2 teaspoon pure almond extract
- 1 1/2 pounds confectioners' sugar, sifted

Direction

- Preheat the oven to 325 degrees F.
- In the bowl of an electric mixer fitted with the paddle attachment, cream the butter and sugar on high speed until light and fluffy, about 5 minutes. With the mixer on low speed, add the eggs, 1 at a time, scraping down the bowl after each addition. Add the vanilla and almond extracts and mix well.
- In a separate bowl, sift together the flour, baking powder, baking soda, and salt. In 3 parts, alternately add the dry ingredients and the buttermilk to the batter, beginning and ending with the dry. Mix until just combined. Fold in 7 ounces of coconut.
- Line a muffin pan with paper liners. Fill each liner to the top with batter. Bake for 25 to 35 minutes, until the tops are brown and a toothpick comes out clean. (Mini cupcakes took about 20 mins in my oven) Allow to cool in the pan for 15 minutes. Remove to a baking rack and cool completely.
- Meanwhile, make the frosting. In the bowl of an electric mixer fitted with the paddle attachment, on low speed, cream together the cream cheese, butter, and vanilla and almond extracts. Add the confectioners' sugar and mix until smooth.
- Frost the cupcakes and sprinkle with the remaining coconut.

101. Irish Car Bomb Cupcakes Recipe

Serving: 24 | Prep: | Cook: 17mins | Ready in:

Ingredients

- For the Cupcakes:
- 1 cup Guinness
- 1 cup (2 sticks) unsalted butter
- 3/4 cup unsweetened cocoa powder (preferably Dutch-process)
- 2 cups all purpose flour
- 2 cups sugar
- 1 1/2 teaspoons baking soda
- 3/4 teaspoon salt
- 2 large eggs
- 2/3 cup sour cream
- Ganache Filling :
- 8 ounces bittersweet chocolate
- 2/3 cup heavy cream
- 2 tablespoons butter, room temperature
- 1 to 2 teaspoons Irish whiskey (optional)
- Baileys frosting (see Notes)
- 3 to 4 cups confections sugar
- 1 stick (1/2 cup or 4 ounces) unsalted butter, at room temperature
- 3 to 4 tablespoons Baileys (or milk, or heavy cream, or a combination thereof)
- You will need 1-inch round cookie cutter or an apple corer and a piping bag (though a plastic bag with the corner snipped off will also work)

Direction

- Make the cupcakes: Preheat oven to 350°F. Line 24 cupcake cups with liners. Bring 1 cup stout and 1 cup butter to simmer in heavy large saucepan over medium heat. Add cocoa powder and whisk until mixture is smooth. Cool slightly.
- Whisk flour, sugar, baking soda, and 3/4 teaspoon salt in large bowl to blend. Using electric mixer, beat eggs and sour cream in another large bowl to blend. Add stout-chocolate mixture to egg mixture and beat just to combine. Add flour mixture and beat briefly on slow speed. Using rubber spatula, fold batter until completely combined. Divide batter among cupcake liners, filling them 2/3 to 3/4 of the way. Bake cake until tester inserted into centre comes out clean, rotating them once front to back if your oven bakes unevenly, about 17 minutes. Cool cupcakes on a rack completely.
- Make the filling: Chop the chocolate and transfer it to a heatproof bowl. Heat the cream until simmering and pour it over the chocolate. Let it sit for one minute and then stir until smooth. (If this has not sufficiently

melted the chocolate, you can return it to a double-boiler to gently melt what remains. ADD THE BUTTER!!!! The alcohol is optional.
- Fill the cupcakes: Let the ganache cool until thick but still soft enough to be piped (the fridge will speed this along but you must stir it every 10 minutes). Meanwhile, using your 1-inch round cookie cutter or an apple corer, cut the centres out of the cooled cupcakes. You want to go most of the way down the cupcake but not cut through the bottom — aim for 2/3 of the way. A slim spoon or grapefruit knife will help you get the centre out. Those are your "tasters". Put the ganache into a piping bag with a wide tip and fill the holes in each cupcake to the top.
- Make the frosting: Whip the butter in the bowl of an electric mixer, or with a hand mixer, for several minutes. You want to get it very light and fluffy.
- Slowly add the powdered sugar, a few tablespoons at a time.
- When the frosting looks thick enough to spread, drizzle in the Baileys (or milk) and whip it until combined. If this has made the frosting too thin (it shouldn't, but just in case) beat in another spoonful or two of powdered sugar.
- Ice and decorate the cupcakes. I like shaving chocolate for the tops.
- I add an Irish flag attached to a toothpick!!!!

102. Key Lime Blossoms Recipe

Serving: 36 | Prep: | Cook: 15mins | Ready in:

Ingredients

- For the muffins:
- 1 box of yellow cake mix
- 1 small box of lemon instant Jello pudding
- 4 large eggs
- 3/4 cup of light vegetable oil
- Glaze:
- 4 cups of powdered sugar
- 1/3 cup of key lime juice or fresh lime juice
- 3 TB veg. oil
- 3 TB water
- MINI MUFFIN PAN
- Wire Rack over a pan covered in foil or wax paper to catch excess glaze.

Direction

- Using a mixer, blend the four ingredients together for the muffins.
- Let this mix at a medium speed for three minutes until well blended.
- The batter will be very thick!
- Spray a mini muffin pan with non-stick spray.
- Using 2 spoons, fill the muffin tins to 1/2.
- Bake at 350 degrees for 12-15 minutes.
- When you remove the pan out of the oven, flip over the muffins on to a dish towel and glaze... see glazing instructions below.
- Glazing
- Mix all of the Glaze ingredients together with a whisk until the mixture is smooth and well-blended.
- Drop two muffins at a time into the glaze and with two forks, move the muffins around in the glaze to cover the muffins completely. Remove the muffins from the glaze and place on the wire rack to dry.
- Once the glaze has dried completely, serve.
- Note: I tried this with orange juice and the muffins were just wonderful. I did use the lemon pudding mixture with the orange muffins. ...... For a more adult flavour, I'm sure you could use a Margherita Mix!

103. Key Lime Cupcakes Recipe

Serving: 24 | Prep: | Cook: 19mins | Ready in:

Ingredients

- Topping
  1 box [4 serving size] vanilla instant pudding and pie filling mix
- 1 1/2 cups whipping cream
- 1/4 cup key lime or regular lime juice
- 4 drops green food color
- 1 1/2 cups powdered sugar
- Cupcakes
- 1 box Betty Crocker super moist yellow cake mix.
- water,vegetable oil and eggs called for on cake mix box.
- frosting
- 1 container Betty Crocker Whipped fluffy white frosting
- 1 Tbsp. key lime or regular lime juice
- 1/2 tsp. grated key lime or regular lime peel.
- 1.In large bowl,beat pudding mix and whipping cream with wire whisk 2 minutes.Let stand 3 minutes.Beat in1/4 cup key lime juice and the food color:stir in powdered sugar until smooth.Cover; refrigerate.
- 2.Heat oven to 375*F [350*F for dark or nonstick pans].Place paper baking cup in each of 24 regular size muffin cups. Make cake batter as directed on box.Spoon about 1 rounded Tbsp. of batter into each muffin cup,using about half of the batter.[Muffin cups will be about 1/3 full] Refrigerate remaining batter.Bake 12 to 16 minutes or until toothpick inserted in center comes out clean.Remove from pan to cooling rack.Repeat with batter.cool cupcakes completely about 15 minutes.
- 3.Remove paper baking cups from cupcakes.Swirl about 2 tsps. of topping on top of each cupcake.
- 4.Stir frosting in container 20 times.Gently stir in 1 Tbsp.key lime juice and the lime peel.Spoon frosting into 1 quart resealable food storage plastic bag.Cut1/2 inch opening from bottom corner of bag.Squeeze 1 rounded teaspoonful frosting onto topping.Garnish with fresh lime wedge if desired.Store in refrigerater.

Direction

- Above

104. Lemon Blossoms Little Cupcakes Recipe

Serving: 24 | Prep: | Cook: 12mins | Ready in:

Ingredients

- 1 yellow cake mix
- 4 eggs
- 1 box lemon pudding
- 3/4 cup oil
- ---------
- glaze
- ---
- 1 box confectionary sugar
- 3 tbsp water
- 1 tblsp lemon zest
- 1/3 cup lemon juice
- 3 tblsp oil

Direction

- Mix all of the above and beat 2-3 minutes
- Fill small muffin pans half full
- Bake at 350 degrees F for approx. 12 minute
- GLAZE
- Combine all of the ingredients and dip top of muffins into glaze and set aside

105. Lemon Blossoms Recipe

Serving: 24 | Prep: | Cook: 15mins | Ready in:

Ingredients

- 18 1/2-ounce package yellow cake mix
- 3 1/2-ounce package instant lemon pudding mix
- 4 large eggs

- 3/4 cup vegetable oil
- Glaze:
- 4 cups confectioners' sugar
- 1/3 cup fresh lemon juice
- 1 lemon, zested
- 3 tablespoons vegetable oil
- 3 tablespoons water

Direction

- Preheat the oven to 350 degrees F.
- Spray miniature muffin tins with vegetable oil cooking spray. Combine the cake mix, pudding mix, eggs and oil and blend well with an electric mixer until smooth, about 2 minutes. Pour a small amount of batter, filling each muffin tin half way.
- Bake for 12 minutes. Turn out onto a tea towel.
- To make the glaze, sift the sugar into a mixing bowl. Add the lemon juice, zest, oil, and 3 tablespoons water. Mix with a spoon until smooth.
- With fingers, dip the cupcakes into the glaze while they're still warm, covering as much of the cake as possible, or spoon the glaze over the warm cupcakes, turning them to completely coat. Place on wire racks with waxed paper underneath to catch any drips. Let the glaze set thoroughly, about 1 hour, before storing in containers with tight-fitting lids.

106. Lemon Butterfly Cupcakes Recipe

Serving: 12 | Prep: | Cook: 25mins | Ready in:

Ingredients

- CUPCAKES
- 1 cup unsalted butter, soften
- 1 1/2 cups sugar
- 4 eggs
- 1 tablespoon vanilla
- 1 tablespoon lemon zest
- 2 tablespoons lemon juice
- 2 1/2 cups flour
- 1 tablespoon baking powder
- 1/4 teaspoon baking soda
- 1/4 salt
- 1 cup buttermilk
- Butterflies:
- 1 cup whipping cream
- 1/2 cup strawberry jam
- 18 blueberries
- 18 thin slices of strawberries
- icing sugar for dusting

Direction

- Preheat the oven to 350. Line muffin pans with paper muffin cups.
- In large bowl, cream butter and sugar together. Add eggs, one at a time, and beat well after each addition. Add vanilla, lemon juice and lemon zest and beat until combined.
- In a large bowl, whisk together flour, baking powder, baking soda and salt. Set aside.
- Beat in flour in 3 additions, alternating with the buttermilk.
- Fill the muffin cups equally. You can fill the muffin cups so it almost comes up to the top. With the back of a spoon, smooth the tops so the cupcakes cooks evenly.
- Bake at 350 for 20 minutes or until the tops start to turn golden and a toothpick inserted in the centre of the cupcakes comes out clean. Let them cool in the muffin pans for 5 minutes, then remove them from the muffin pans to cool completely on a wire rack.
- Whip the cream to firm peaks. Using a sharp knife, cut shallow rounds from the top of each cupcake. Cut these rounds in half; these will be the butterfly wings. Spoon a teaspoon of strawberry jam into the cavity of each cupcake top. Cover the jam with a dollop of whipped cream.
- Place a strawberry slice on top of the whipped cream to form the body. Add a blueberry at the top of the strawberry slice to form the head. Position two halves of cupcake tops on

either side of the strawberry to resemble butterfly wings.
- Dust the cupcakes with icing sugar before serving.

107. Lemon Cream Cheese Cupcakes Recipe

Serving: 24 | Prep: | Cook: 24mins | Ready in:

Ingredients

- 1 pkg. (2 layer size) white cake mix
- 1 pkg. (4 serving size) lemon flavor instant pudding and pie filling
- 1 cup water
- 4 egg whites
- 2 Tbsp. oil
- 1 pkg. (16-oz.) powdered sugar
- 1 pkg. (8-oz.) cream cheese, softened
- 1/4 cup butter, softened
- 2 Tbsp. lemon juice

Direction

- Preheat the oven to 350*F.
- Beat cake mix and dry pudding mix, water, egg whites and oil in large bowl with electric mixer on low speed until moistened. (Batter will be thick)
- Beat on medium speed 2 minutes.
- Spoon batter evenly into 24 paper lined (2-1/2") muffin cups.
- Bake 24 minutes or until wooden toothpick inserted in centres comes out clean.
- Cool in pans 10 minutes on wire racks, remove and cool completely.
- Meanwhile beat sugar, cream cheese, butter and juice with an electric mixer on low speed until well blended.
- Frost cooled muffins.

108. Lemon Meringue Cupcakes From The Culinary Institute Of America Recipe

Serving: 24 | Prep: | Cook: 20mins | Ready in:

Ingredients

- lemon Chiffon Cupcakes
- 3 cups cake flour
- 2 teaspoons baking powder
- 1 cup sugar, divided
- 4 large egg yolks
- 1 cup vegetable oil
- 1 cup water
- 1/2 teaspoon vanilla extract
- Zest of 1 lemon
- 4 large egg whites
- ....
- lemon curd
- 1 cup butter, cubed
- 1 cup sugar
- 1 cup lemon juice
- Zest of 3 lemons
- 10 large egg yolks
- ....
- Swiss Meringue buttercream
- 4 large egg whites
- 1 cup sugar

Direction

- Prepare the Lemon Chiffon Cupcakes.
- Preheat the oven to 375°F. Prepare pans with cupcake liners. Sift the flour, baking powder, and half the sugar together into a large mixing bowl or stand mixer and reserve. In another large mixing bowl or stand mixer bowl, combine the egg yolks, oil, water, vanilla, and zest. Mix with a handheld mixer or whip attachment until thoroughly combined, about 1 minute. Add the egg yolk mixture gradually to the dry ingredients, mixing with a handheld mixer or whip attachment on medium speed until a paste forms. When a paste has formed, scrape down the sides of the bowl, and continue adding the remainder of the yolk

mixture until it is all incorporated. Beat for an additional 2 minutes on medium speed. In a separate mixing bowl or stand mixer bowl, whip the egg whites with a clean whip attachment on medium speed until soft peaks form. Gradually add the remaining sugar while beating the egg whites and continue to beat until medium peaks form. Gently blend one-third of the beaten egg whites into the egg yolk mixture to lighten it. Gently fold in the remaining egg whites. Divide the batter evenly among the prepared pans. Bake at 375°F until the top of the cupcakes spring back to the touch, about 20 minutes. Let the cupcakes cool in the pans for a few minutes before turning out onto a wire rack to finish cooling before decorating.

- ....
- Prepare Lemon Curd.
- Combine half of the butter, half of the sugar, the lemon juice, and zest and bring to a boil over medium heat, stirring gently to dissolve the sugar. Meanwhile, blend the egg yolks with the remaining sugar. Temper the mixture by gradually adding about one-third of the lemon juice mixture, stirring constantly with a whip. Return the tempered egg mixture to the saucepan. Continue cooking, stirring constantly, until the whisk leaves a trail in the curd. Remove from the heat. Stir in the remaining butter. Strain the curd into a shallow container or bowl. Cover with plastic wrap placed directly on the surface of the curd. Cool over an ice bath. Store the curd, covered, in the refrigerator for up to 3 days.
- ....
- Prepare Swiss Meringue Buttercream.
- Put the egg whites and sugar in the clean, grease-free bowl of a stand mixer fitted with the whisk attachment and stir together until the sugar is blended into the egg whites. Place the bowl over a saucepan of simmering water and stir frequently until the sugar dissolves and the mixture reaches 140°F. Transfer the bowl to the mixer and beat on high speed until the meringue is thick and glossy and has a stiff peak.
- ....
- Finish the cupcakes.
- Fill a piping bag fitted with a large plain tip two-thirds full with lemon curd. Insert the tip as far as it will go inside the centre of the cupcake and apply gentle pressure. Try not to squeeze too hard or lemon curd will squirt out the top of the cupcake. Stop filling once you see any lemon curd around the base of the tip. Repeat with the remaining cupcakes. Clean the piping bag and tip and fill it two-thirds full with Swiss meringue. Pipe a large pearl of meringue on top of each cupcake. Use the back of a spoon to lift up areas of the meringue, creating spikes. Lightly toast the meringue with a kitchen torch or under the broiler until the tips of the meringue are golden brown.

109. Lemon Raspberry Cupcakes Recipe

Serving: 12 | Prep: | Cook: 80mins | Ready in:

Ingredients

- 3/4c(11/2 sticks) unsalted butter,room temperature
- 3c powdered sugar,divided
- 41/2tsp finely grated lemon peel,divided
- 2 large eggs
- 11/4c self rising flour
- 1/4c buttermilk
- 4Tbs fresh lemon juice,divided
- 12tsp. plus 1 Tbs. seedless raspberry jam
- fresh raspberries for garnish

Direction

- Preheat oven to 350. Line 12 muffin cups with paper liners. Using electric mixer, beat butter, 11/2 cups powdered sugar and 3 tsp. lemon peel in a large bowl till blended; then beat

until fluffy and pale yellow. Add eggs one at a time, beating to blend after each addition. Beat in half of flour. Add buttermilk and 2 Tbs. lemon juice; beat to blend Beat in remaining flour.
- Drop 1 rounded tbs. batter into each muffin liner. Spoon 1tsp raspberry jam over. Cover with remaining batter, dividing equally.
- Bake cupcakes until tester inserted halfway into centres comes out clean, about 23 mins. Cool cupcakes in pan on rack. Meanwhile, whisk remaining 1 1/2c powdered sugar, 2Tbsp. lemon juice, and 1 1/2tsp. lemon peel in small bowl. Spoon 1/2 of icing over 6 cupcakes. Whisk 1Tbs raspberry jam into remaining icing. Spoon over remaining cupcakes. Let stand till icing sets, about 30 mins. Garnish with raspberries.

110. Light Carrot Cake Cupcakes With Cream Cheese Frosting Recipe

Serving: 0 | Prep: | Cook: 25mins | Ready in:

Ingredients

- For the Cupcakes
- * 1 C whole wheat flour
- * 1 1/2 C all-purpose flour
- * 1 1/2 C grated carrots
- * 1 tsp baking powder
- * 1 tsp baking soda
- * 1/4 tsp ground allspice
- * 1/4 tsp ground nutmeg
- * 1/4 tsp ground cinnamon
- * 1/2 tsp salt
- * 1 1/3 C sugar or 1/2 C sugar substitute and 1/2 C sugar
- * 1/4 C dark brown sugar
- * 3 eggs
- * 1 C non-fat plain yogurt
- * 1/4 C unsweetened applesauce
- * 1/4 C canola oil

- For the frosting
- * 1 8oz package of 1/3 of the fat cream cheese, softened
- * 2 tbsp butter, room temperature
- * 1 1/2 tsp vanilla extract
- * pinch of salt
- * 2 C confectioner's sugar, sifted

Direction

- 1. Preheat oven to 350. Place cupcake liners in muffins tins.
- 2. Place grated carrots into a large mixing bowl and set aside.
- 3. Put flours, sugars, baking powder, baking soda, allspice, nutmeg, cinnamon, and salt into the bowl of a food processor or stand mixer. Pulse or mix for about for about 10 seconds. Add the flour mixture to the grated carrots and toss to coat.
- 4. Next add the sugars, eggs, yogurt, and applesauce to the bowl of the food processor/stand mixer and pulse/beat until creamy. Add in the oil and mix until well-combined.
- 5. Pour the sugar mixture in the carrots and stir until just moistened.
- 6. Fill cupcake liners about 2/3 full and bake for 20-30 minutes or until toothpick inserted into the centre comes out clean.
- 7. Remove cupcakes to wire rack and allow to cool completely.
- Preparing the Frosting
- 1. Using a stand mixer, beat cream cheese and butter together until blended. Add in the vanilla and salt and beat until smooth. Add in the confectioner's sugar a 1/2 cup at a time and beat until smooth and creamy.
- 2. Refrigerate for at least 10 minutes before frosting cupcakes.
- 3. Store leftover cupcakes in refrigerator.

111. Little Lemon Yogurt Puffs Recipe

Serving: 12 | Prep: | Cook: 12mins | Ready in:

Ingredients

- 1 egg
- 1 egg white
- 1/2 cup low-fat lemon yogurt
- 1/3 cup sugar
- 1 tsp vanilla
- zest of 1 lemon
- juice of 1/2 lemon
- 2 tbsp olive oil
- 1 1/4 cups flour
- 1 tsp baking powder
- 1/4 tsp baking soda

Direction

- Preheat oven to 350F, grease 10 mini-muffin cups or line with paper liners.
- In a bowl, beat together egg, egg white, yogurt, sugar, vanilla, lemon zest, lemon juice and olive oil. Set aside.
- In another bowl, whisk together flour, baking powder and baking soda.
- Add dry mixture to the wet ingredients, stirring quickly but gently just to combine.
- Spoon into muffin cups.
- Bake 12-15 minutes, until test done. Turn out immediately and cool on a rack.

112. Little Sacher Cupcakes Recipe

Serving: 12 | Prep: | Cook: 15mins | Ready in:

Ingredients

- 1 1/4 cup all-purpose flour
- 1/3 cup granulated sugar
- 1/3 cup ground almonds (about 1 1/2 ounces)
- 1/2 teaspoon baking powder
- 1/2 teaspoon baking soda
- 1/4 teaspoon salt
- 6 tablespoons (3/4 stick) butter, softened
- 2/3 cup firmly packed light brown sugar
- 2 large eggs
- 1/2 cup milk
- 2 ounces (2 squares) unsweetened chocolate, melted
- 1 tablespoon rum or 1 teaspoon rum extract
- 1/2 cup apricot preserves, melted
- For the Glaze:
- 2/3 cup heavy cream
- 6 ounces (6 squares) semisweet chocolate, coarsely chopped
- 2 tablespoons butter
- 2 tablespoons light corn syrup
- For the Topping and Garnish:
- whipped cream
- candied violets

Direction

- Preheat oven to 350F. Grease 12 standard size muffin-pan cups or line with paper liners. Dust with flour; tap out excess.
- Mix together flour, granulated sugar, nuts, baking powder, baking soda, and salt.
- Beat together butter and brown sugar at medium speed until light and fluffy. Add eggs, 1 at a time, beating well after each addition. At low speed, beat in milk, melted chocolate, and rum. Beat flour mixture into milk mixture until combined. Spoon batter into prepared pan, filling cups three-quarters full.
- Bake cupcakes until a toothpick inserted in the centre comes out clean, 15 minutes. Transfer pan to a wire rack to cool for 10 minutes. Turn cupcakes out onto rack to cool completely.
- Brush melted preserves over cupcakes. Let stand until set, 30 minutes.
- To prepare glaze, in a medium saucepan, heat cream, chocolate, butter, and corn syrup over medium heat, stirring constantly, until chocolate melts and mixture boils. Remove from heat; let stand for 1 minute. Stir

vigorously until mixture thickens. Spread glaze evenly over cupcakes. Let stand until set.
- Suggestion:
- Using a pastry bag fitted with a star tip, pipe whipped cream rosettes on top. Garnish with a candied violet in the centre of each rosette.

113. Magnolia Bakery Red Velvet Cupcakes Recipe

Serving: 36 | Prep: | Cook: 40mins | Ready in:

Ingredients

- 3 ⅓ cups cake flour (not self-rising)
- ¾ cup (1 ½ sticks) unsalted butter, softened
- 2 ¼ cups sugar
- 3 large eggs, at room temperature
- 6 tablespoons red food coloring
- 3 tablespoons unsweetened cocoa
- 1 ½ teaspoons vanilla extract
- 1 ½ teaspoons salt
- 1 ½ cups buttermilk
- 1 ½ teaspoons cider vinegar
- 1 ½ teaspoons baking soda
- Frosting: 1 pound (two 8-ounce packages) cream cheese, softened and cut into small pieces
- 6 tablespoons unsalted butter, softened and cut into small pieces
- 1 ½ teaspoons vanilla extract
- 5 cups sifted confectioners' sugar

Direction

- Preheat oven to 350 degrees.
- Grease and lightly flour three muffin tins. Place cupcake papers in the tins.
- To make the cake: In a small bowl, sift the cake flour and set aside. In a large bowl, on the medium speed of an electric mixer, cream the butter and sugar until very light and fluffy, about 5 minutes. Add the eggs, one at a time, beating well after each addition.
- In a small bowl, whisk together the red food colouring, cocoa, and vanilla. Add to the batter and beat well.
- In a measuring cup, stir the salt into the buttermilk. Add to the batter in three parts, alternating with the flour. With each addition, beat until the ingredients are incorporated, but do not overheat.
- In a small bowl, stir together the cider vinegar and baking soda. Add to the batter and mix well. Using a rubber spatula, scrape down the batter in the bowl, making sure the ingredients are well blended and the batter is smooth.
- Divide the batter among the prepared pans. Bake each tray for 20 minutes, or until a cake tester inserted in the centre of the cake comes out clean. Let the cupcakes cool in the pans for 1 hour. Remove from the pans and cool completely on a wire rack.
- Frosting: In a large bowl, on the medium speed of an electric mixer, beat the cream cheese and butter until smooth, about 3 minutes.
- Add the vanilla and beat well.
- Gradually add the sugar, 1 cup at a time, beating continuously until smooth and creamy.
- Cover and refrigerate icing for 2 to 3 hours, but no longer, to thicken before using.
- When the cake has cooled, spread the frosting liberally on the cupcakes.
- Makes 36 cupcakes.

114. Mandarin Orange Frosty Recipe

Serving: 8 | Prep: | Cook: | Ready in:

Ingredients

- 1- can (11 ounces) mandarin oranges drained
- 1- can (8 ounces) crushed pineapple drained
- 1- cup vanilla low-fat yogurt
- 1- cup miniature marshmallows

- 1/2- cup drained and chopped maraschino cherries
- baking paper cups

Direction

- Combine all ingredients in a large
- Spoon into muffin cups lined with baking cups (you can make this miniature too for a party)
- Freeze for 6 hours until solid
- Remove from freezer, peel off baking cups
- Let stand 10 minutes and serve........ Yummy.......
- Serves 8
- *****************
- Note:
- The great thing about this it's so darn easy and the kids or grandkids can make this easily!!!

115. Margarita Cupcakes Recipe

Serving: 24 | Prep: | Cook: 25mins | Ready in:

Ingredients

- CUPCAKE INGREDIENTS
- 1 package (18.25 oz. white cake mix (no pudding in the mix)
- 1 can (10 oz.) frozen margarita mix, thawed (undiluted)
- 3 egg whites
- 2 tablespoons vegetable oil
- 1 tablespoon grated lime zest
- KEY lime cream cheese icing INGREDIENTS
- 8 tablespoons (1 stick) unsalted butter, softened
- 1 package (8 oz.) cream cheese, softened
- 2 tablespoons key lime juice
- 1 teaspoon key lime zest or lemon zest
- 4-5 cups confectioners' sugar

Direction

- Preheat oven to 350° F. Line standard muffin pan with baking cups.
- In large bowl, combine cake mix, Margarita mix, egg whites and vegetable oil using electric mixer.
- Stir in lime zest; mix completely.
- Fill prepared pans 2/3 full.
- Bake 22-24 minutes or until toothpick inserted in centre of cupcake comes out clean.
- Cool in pan on cooling rack 5-8 minutes.
- Remove cupcakes from pan; cool completely.
- Frost cooled cupcakes with icing and garnish, if desired, with a strawberry and/or lime twist.
- ICING DIRECTIONS
- In large bowl, cream butter, cream cheese, juice and zest with electric mixer until light and fluffy.
- Add 4 cups confectioners' sugar, one cup at a time; continue beating until light and fluffy.
- If icing is too thin add additional confectioners' sugar 1 tablespoon at a time.

116. Mexi Late Cupcakes Recipe

Serving: 12 | Prep: | Cook: 20mins | Ready in:

Ingredients

- 1/3 cup butter
- 1/4 cup cocoa powder
- 1/3 cup water
- 1/2 cup granulated sugar
- 1/4 cup dark brown sugar
- 1 egg
- 1/4 cup buttermilk
- 2 tbsp vanilla
- 1 1/2 cups all purpose flour
- 1/2 cup rolled oats
- 1/2 tsp baking soda
- 1 tsp cinnamon
- pinch cayenne pepper
- pinch salt

Direction

- Preheat oven to 350. Grease 12 muffin cups.
- Melt butter and whisk in the cocoa.
- Add water, stirring until smooth then remove from heat.
- Stir sugar, eggs, buttermilk, and vanilla in until thoroughly blended.
- Mix together flour, oats, baking soda, cinnamon, cayenne and salt.
- Stir into the cocoa mixture and whisk until just combined (it will be a little bit lumpy).
- Fill tins almost all the way full.
- Bake for 20 minutes.

117. Mini OREO Surprise Cupcakes Recipe

Serving: 24 | Prep: | Cook: 19mins | Ready in:

Ingredients

- 1 pkg. (2-layer size) chocolate cake mix
- 1 pkg. (8 oz.) PHILADELPHIA cream cheese, softened
- 1 egg
- 2 Tbsp. sugar
- 48 Mini OREO Bite Size chocolate Sandwich cookies 1-1/2 cups thawed Cool Whip whipped topping

Direction

- PREHEAT oven to 350°F. Prepare cake batter in large mixing bowl as directed on package; set aside.
- WHISK cream cheese, egg and sugar in small mixing bowl until well blended.
- SCOOP cake batter, using 1/4-cup dry measuring cup, into each of 24 paper or foil-lined medium muffin cups, filling each cup about half full.
- SPOON 1/2 Tbsp. of cream cheese mixture over batter in each muffin cup. Top with 1 cookie. Cover evenly with remaining cake batter.
- BAKE 19 to 22 minutes or until toothpick inserted in centre comes out clean. Cool 5 minutes; remove from pans to wire racks. Cool completely.
- TOP cupcakes with whipped topping and remaining cookies just before serving. Makes 24 servings.

118. Mini Oreo Cupcakes Recipe

Serving: 24 | Prep: | Cook: 22mins | Ready in:

Ingredients

- 1 pkg (2 layer size) chocolate cake mix
- 1 pkg cream cheese, softened (8 oz; 250 g)
- 1 egg
- 2 tbsp sugar (30 ml)
- 48 mini bite size Oreo cookies
- 1 - 1 1/2 cup icing, or whipped cream

Direction

- Prepare batter as directed on package.
- Set aside.
- Beat cream cheese, egg and sugar until well blended.
- Spoon batter into muffin cups or muffin pan, filling each cup about half full.
- Top each with about 1- 1 1/2 tsp. of the cream cheese.
- Put a cookie on top.
- Cover evenly with the remaining cake batter.
- Bake at 350 degrees F (160 degrees C) for 19 t0 22 minutes.
- Cool 5 minutes.
- Remove from pans to wire racks.
- Cool completely.
- Top cupcakes with icing or cream and remaining cookies.
- Serve

119. Mucho Mocha Berry Cupcakes Recipe

Serving: 12 | Prep: | Cook: 20mins | Ready in:

Ingredients

- 1 cup whole wheat pastry flour
- ½ cup brown rice flour
- ½ cup unsweetened cocoa powder
- 1 ½ teaspoons baking powder
- ½ teaspoon baking soda
- ¼ teaspoon salt
- ¾ cup strong coffee, hot
- ¼ cup pure maple syrup
- 1 tbsp canola oil
- ¼ cup thick, unsweetened apple butter
- 1 tablespoon rice wine vinegar
- 1 teaspoon almond extract
- ½ teaspoon vanilla extract
- 1/2 cup slivered almonds
- 1 cup raspberries, processed until slightly chunky
- powdered sugar (optional)

Direction

- Preheat oven to 325°F, grease 12 muffin cups.
- In a large bowl, combine flours, cocoa, baking powder, baking soda, and salt.
- In a small bowl, mix coffee, syrup, oil, apple butter, vinegar, and extracts.
- Add wet ingredients to dry and stir until almost completely blended. Do not beat.
- Add almonds and raspberries and fold in until incorporated.
- Bake for 20 minutes.
- Let cool for 10 minutes, remove from pan, and sprinkle with powdered sugar if desired.

120. Nana Nog Cupcakes Recipe

Serving: 8 | Prep: | Cook: 20mins | Ready in:

Ingredients

- 1/2 cup (1.7 oz) flour
- 2 tbsp (0.6 oz) whole wheat flour
- 3 tbsp (1 oz) vanilla custard powder
- 1 1/2 tsp baking powder
- 1/4 tsp nutmeg
- 1/4 tsp salt
- 3 3/4 tbsp (2 oz) low-fat (not fat free) cream cheese, softened
- 1 1/2 tbsp (0.7 oz) low-fat margarine
- 7 tbsp (3 oz) sugar
- 1 banana, mashed
- 1/2 tbsp vanilla
- 1/4 cup egg nog
- 1/4 cup (1.5 oz) white chocolate chips

Direction

- Preheat oven to 400F, grease 9 muffin cups with non-stick spray (I don't recommend lining them - they stick).
- In a small bowl, whisk together flours, custard powder, baking powder, nutmeg and salt. Set aside.
- In a medium-large bowl, cream cream cheese, margarine and sugar.
- Add banana and vanilla, beat well to combine.
- Stir in half the flour mixture, followed by the eggnog.
- Add the remaining flour mixture and white chocolate chips mixing well.
- Bake for 17-18 minutes.
- Cool 5 minutes in the tins before turning out and cooling completely.

121. Nigellas Lavendar Cupcakes Recipe

Serving: 12 | Prep: | Cook: 20mins | Ready in:

Ingredients

- FOR THE CUPCAKES:
- 125g self-raising flour
- 125g very soft unsalted butter
- 125g lavender sugar, sieved
- 2 eggs
- pinch salt
- few tablespoons milk
- FOR THE ICING:
- 250g Instant Royal icing powder
- violet food colouring paste
- handful real lavender stalks

Direction

- Preheat the oven to 200°C/gas mark 6 and line a 12-bun cupcake or muffin tin with paper cases. Take butter, eggs and milk out of the fridge in time to make sure they're at room temperature.
- Put all the ingredients for the cupcakes, except for the milk, into the bowl of a food processor, fitted with a double-bladed knife, and blitz till totally combined. Process again, adding enough milk to make a batter with a smooth, flowing texture, then remove the blade and spoon and scrape the batter equally into the waiting cupcake cases.
- Bake for about 20 minutes, by which time the sponge should be cooked through and springy to the touch. Remove from the oven, leave for 5 minutes or so, and then arrange the cupcakes in their paper cases on a wire rack to cool.
- Once they're cool, you can get on with the icing. You want the icing to sit thickly on the cupcakes not run off them, and you can aid this by cutting off any risen humps with a sharp knife first, so that each cake is flat-topped.
- Make the icing and dye the mixture a faint lilac with a spot or two of food colouring.
- Top each pretty-pale cupcake with a little sprig of lavender before the icing's set dry.

122. No Bake Chocolate Cream Cupcakes Recipe

Serving: 2 | Prep: | Cook: 110mins | Ready in:

Ingredients

- 1/2 cup thawed Cool Whip whipped topping, divided 2 oz.
- (1/4 of 8-oz. pkg.) PHILADELPHIA cream cheese, softened
- 1 square BAKER'S Semi-Sweet baking chocolate, melted, cooled
- 1 Tbsp. powdered sugar
- 8 NILLA Wafers

Direction

- MIX 1/4 cup of the whipped topping, the cream cheese, melted chocolate and sugar until well blended.
- PLACE 2 of the wafers in bottom of each of 2 paper-lined medium muffin cups. Cover with 1 Tbsp. of the whipped topping mixture. Repeat layers. Top evenly with remaining whipped topping. Cover.
- REFRIGERATE at least 1 hour.

123. Nonnas Lemon Ricotta Biscuits Recipe

Serving: 12 | Prep: | Cook: 20mins | Ready in:

Ingredients

- 2 cups all-purpose flour
- 1/2 tsp baking powder
- 1/2 tsp baking soda
- 1/2 tsp salt

- 1 cup granulated sugar, plus more for sprinkling
- 1/2 cup unsalted butter, at room temperature
- 1 Tbsp finely grated lemon zest (from 2 lemons)
- 1 cup whole-milk ricotta cheese
- 1 large egg
- 1 Tbsp fresh lemon juice
- 1/2 tsp almond extract
- 1/3 cup thinly sliced almonds

Direction

- Line 12 muffin cups with paper liners.
- Preheat oven to 350 degrees.
- Whisk the flour, baking powder, baking soda, and salt in a medium bowl to blend.
- In a large bowl, using an electric mixer, beat 1 cup sugar, butter, and lemon zest until light and fluffy.
- Beat in the ricotta.
- Beat in egg, lemon juice, and almond extract.
- Add the dry ingredients and stir just until blended (the batter will be thick and fluffy).
- Divide the batter among the prepared muffin cups.
- Sprinkle the almonds and some sugar over the muffins.
- Bake until the muffins just become pale golden on top, about 20 minutes.
- Cool slightly.
- Serve warm or at room temperature.

124. Nutella Self Frosting Cupcakes Recipe

Serving: 12 | Prep: | Cook: 20mins | Ready in:

Ingredients

- 10 tbsp butter, softened
- 3/4 cup white sugar
- 3 eggs
- 1/2 tsp vanilla
- 1 3/4 cups sifted flour
- 1/4 tsp salt
- 2 tsp baking powder
- 1/3 cup nutella

Direction

- Preheat oven to 325F. Line 12 muffin tins with paper liners.
- Cream together butter and sugar.
- Add in eggs one at a time, until fully incorporated.
- Add vanilla.
- Stir in flour, salt and baking powder until batter is uniform and no flour remains.
- Using a scoop, fill each muffin liner 3/4 full with batter.
- Top each cake with 1 1/2 tsp. Nutella.
- Swirl Nutella in with a toothpick, making sure to fold a bit of batter up over the Nutella.
- Bake for 20 minutes.
- Remove to a wire rack to cool completely.

125. Nutella Or Peanut Butter Cupcakes Recipe

Serving: 12 | Prep: | Cook: 20mins | Ready in:

Ingredients

- 10 T butter, softened
- 3/4 cup white sugar
- 3 eggs
- 1/2 tsp vanilla
- 1 3/4 cups (200 grams) sifted all purpose flour
- 1/4 tsp salt
- 2 tsp baking powder
- nutella, approx. 1/3 cup

Direction

- Preheat oven to 325
- Line 12 muffin tins with paper liners
- Cream together butter and sugar until light, about 2 minutes

- Add in eggs one at a time, until fully incorporated
- Add vanilla
- Stir in flour, salt and baking powder until batter is uniform
- Fill each muffin cup 3/4 full
- Top each cake with 1 1/2 tsp. Nutella
- Swirl Nutella in with a toothpick, making sure to fold a bit of batter up over the Nutella
- Bake for 20 minutes
- Remove to a wire rack to cool completely

126. Oatmeal Raisin Muffins Recipe

Serving: 12 | Prep: | Cook: 25mins | Ready in:

Ingredients

- 2 cups flour
- 1/2 cup packed light-brown sugar
- 1/2 cup granulated sugar
- 1 tbsp baking powder
- 1/4 tsp allspice
- 3/4 tsp salt
- 1 cup quick-cook oatmeal
- 1/2 cup raisins
- 1/2 cup chopped walnuts
- 1 egg
- 1/2 cup oil
- 1 1/4 cups milk
- 1 tsp vanilla extract

Direction

- 1. Heat oven to 375. Coat 12 muffin cups with non-stick cooking spray.
- 2. In large bowl, whisk together flour, both sugars, baking powder, allspice and salt. Stir in oatmeal, raisins and nuts. In medium-size bowl, lightly beat egg. Stir in oil, milk and vanilla to combine; stir gently into flour mixture; do not over mix.
- 3. Fill muffin cups two-thirds full. Bake at 375 for 25 minutes or until golden on top. Remove to wire rack to cool.

127. Oreo Cupcakes Recipe

Serving: 24 | Prep: | Cook: 20mins | Ready in:

Ingredients

- 2 1/3 cups flour
- 1 cup unsweetened cocoa powder
- 1 1/2 tsp baking powder
- 1/2 tsp baking soda
- 1/2 tsp salt
- 12 tbsp unsalted butter, room temperature
- 2 cups light brown sugar
- 2 tsp vanilla extract
- 4 eggs
- 1 1/2 cups buttermilk
- frosting
- 1 3/4 cup plus 2 tbsp whipping cream
- 3 tbsp powdered sugar
- 1/2 tsp vanilla extract
- 6 tbsp crushed oreos
- 12 Oreos Halfed

Direction

- Preheat oven to 350
- In bowl, mix together flour, cocoa powder, baking soda, baking powder, and salt
- In electric mixer cream butter until smooth
- Add in brown sugar and mix until fluffy
- Add in vanilla and eggs, mixing after each addition
- Slowly add in flour mixture in 3 parts, alternating with addition of buttermilk
- Pour batter into 24 muffin tins
- Bake 18-20 minutes
- In electric mixture, mix whipping cream, powdered sugar, and vanilla extract until stiff
- Once desired consistency, fold in Oreo crumbs
- Once cupcakes have cool, pipe frosting on top of each cupcake

- Break the whole Oreos in half and top each cupcake with half of an Oreo

128. Paula Deens Crispy Rice Cupcakes Recipe

Serving: 9 | Prep: | Cook: 2mins | Ready in:

Ingredients

- 6 tablespoons butter
- 2 (10.5-ounce) packages miniature marshmallows
- 1/2 cup creamy peanut butter
- 2 teaspoons vanilla extract
- 1 (12-ounce) box crispy rice cereal
- 3 (2-ounce) bottles colored sprinkles, divided
- 1 (16-ounce) package chocolate-flavored candy coating
- 4 tablespoons solid vegetable shortening

Direction

- Lightly grease 2 (12-cup) muffin pans.
- In a large saucepan, melt butter over medium heat.
- Add marshmallows, and stir constantly until melted.
- Remove from heat; stir in peanut butter and vanilla.
- Add cereal and 2 bottles sprinkles, stirring until combined.
- Using greased hands, press into prepared pans, mounding mixture into a cupcake shape.
- Cool 1 hour.
- Remove cupcakes from pans.
- In a medium bowl, combine candy coating and vegetable shortening.
- Microwave on High, in 30-second intervals, stirring in between each, until chocolate is melted and smooth (about 2 minutes total time).
- Dip tops of cupcakes in melted chocolate.
- Immediately sprinkle with remaining sprinkles.

129. Peachy Lemon Muffins Recipe

Serving: 12 | Prep: | Cook: 20mins | Ready in:

Ingredients

- muffins:
- 2 cups all purpose flour
- 1/2 cup firmly packed brown sugar
- 1 teaspoon baking powder
- 1/2 teaspoon baking soda
- 1/4 teaspoon salt
- 1 teaspoon cinnamon
- 1/2 teaspoon ground cloves
- 1/2 teaspoon ground ginger
- 3 tablespoons unsalted butter (melted)
- 1-2 teaspoons finely grated lemon zest
- 2-4 tablespoon freshly squeezed lemon juice
- 2 large eggs
- 1 teaspoon vanilla extract
- 8 oz. low-fat yogurt (lemon flavored works best but any will do)
- 2-3 large peaches (cut into chunks, skin on)
- glaze:
- 1/4 cup brown sugar
- 1/4 unsalted butter

Direction

- Muffins:
- Preheat oven to 400 degrees.
- Combine flour, sugar, baking powder and soda, salt, cinnamon, ginger and cloves with a wire whisk until completely combined.
- Make a well in the middle of the dry ingredients.
- Add the butter, zest, juice, eggs, vanilla, and yogurt and stir until just moist.
- Gently fold in the chunky peaches.
- Spray 12 muffin tins with cooking spray and fill each cup full to the top.
- Bake for 20 minutes or until golden brown

- NOTE: my oven tends to run a little low on the temperature gage so I suggest checking the muffins after 15 minutes just to be on the safe side!
- Glaze:
- Combine butter and sugar in a small sauce pan over medium heat just until melted. While muffins are still piping hot brush glaze over each muffin top.

130. Peanut Butter And Jelly Cupcakes Recipe

Serving: 24 | Prep: | Cook: 22mins | Ready in:

Ingredients

- 1 C creamy peanut butter
- 1 1/3 C warm water
- 1 box (1 lb. 2.25 oz.) yellow cake mix
- 3 large eggs
- 2 Tbl. oil
- 1/2 c strawberry jam

Direction

- Heat oven to 350 degrees.
- Line 24 muffin cups with paper or tin foil liners.
- Put peanut butter and water in a large bowl. Beat with mixer on low speed until well blended.
- Add cake mix, eggs and oil; beat on low speed 1 minute to combine. Increase speed to medium and beat 2 minutes or until thickened and smooth.
- Spoon into lined cups.
- Place a tsp. strawberry jam on top middle of each and press jam down slightly with back of spoon.
- Bake 20 to 22 minutes until a wooden pick inserted near centre of cupcakes comes out clean.
- Cool in pan on a wire rack 5 minutes before removing cupcakes from pan to rack to cool completely.

131. Peanut Butter Cup Mousse Cake Recipe

Serving: 12 | Prep: | Cook: 15mins | Ready in:

Ingredients

- cocoa Chiffon Cake:
- 1/2 cup plus 2 tablespoons sifted cake flour
- 1/2 cup plus 3 tablespoons granulated sugar
- 1/3 cup Godiva® Hot cocoa powder, Dark Truffle Flavor, sifted
- 1/2 teaspoon baking powder
- 1/8 teaspoon salt
- 2 eggs plus 3 egg whites, at room temperature
- 1/4 cup plus 2 teaspoons vegetable oil
- 2 teaspoons vanilla extract
- peanut butter Mousse:
- 1 3/4 cups (10 ounces) peanut butter chips
- 3/4 cup whole milk
- 1/2 cup creamy peanut butter
- 1 tablespoon vanilla extract
- 1 cup heavy cream
- 2 tablespoons confectioner's sugar
- milk chocolate Glaze:
- 5 bars (1.5 ounces each) Godiva® milk chocolate, coarsely chopped
- 1/2 cup plus 2 tablespoons heavy cream
- 1 teaspoon vanilla extract
- Garnish
- 1/3 cup unsalted roasted peanuts, finely chopped

Direction

- Make Cake:
- 1. Position rack in centre of oven and preheat to 350°F. Lightly butter bottom and sides of a 9-inch round cake pan. Line with a circle of

baking parchment or waxed paper. Dust side of pan with flour and tap out excess.
- 2. Stir together flour, 1/2 cup sugar, cocoa, baking powder and salt in medium bowl.
- 3. In large bowl, whisk together 2 whole eggs, oil and vanilla until frothy.
- Sift flour mixture over egg mixture and stir until smooth. Mixture will be stiff.
- 4. In a grease-free medium mixer bowl, with the whisk attachment, beat egg whites until frothy. Gradually increase speed to medium-high and continue to beat until they start to form soft peaks. Add remaining sugar, 1 teaspoon at a time. Continue to beat until egg white mixture forms a stiff, shiny meringue.
- 5. Using large rubber spatula, gently fold 1/3 egg white mixture into the egg- flour mixture to lighten it. Fold in remaining egg white mixture. Do not over mix batter. Scrape into prepared pan and spread evenly with a spatula.
- 6. Bake for 15 minutes or until cake springs back when gently touched in centre. Cool cake in pan 5 minutes. Invert to wire rack and cool completely
- Make Mousse:
- 1. Put peanut butter chips into large bowl. In small saucepan, heat milk to a gentle boil. Pour hot milk over peanut butter chips. Let stand 30 seconds. Whisk until smooth and add peanut butter and vanilla. Let stand 5 minutes or until tepid.
- 2. In chilled bowl, beat cream and confectioner's sugar just until soft mounds barely start to form and cream in still pourable. Do not over beat cream. Gently fold 1/3 whipped cream mixture into peanut butter mixture to lighten it. Fold in remaining whipped cream. Do not over mix mousse or it will become grainy.
- Assemble Cake:
- 1. Lightly oil bottom and side of a 9-inch fluted tart pan with removable bottom. Line bottom and sides of pan with plastic wrap, smoothing out any wrinkles, and pressing it into ridges on sides of pan. Scrape peanut butter mousse into pan and spread it in an even layer, filling in all fluted indentations in side of pan with mousse.
- 2. Remove paper circle from bottom of cake. Place cake on top of mousse in tart pan and gently press into place. Cover layer of cake with plastic wrap.
- Freeze for 3 hours or until firm.
- 3. Remove plastic wrap from cake and invert onto a cardboard cake round.
- Lift off side and bottom of tart pan, using a thin bladed knife if necessary
- Peel off plastic wrap from peanut butter mousse layer.
- Make Milk Chocolate Glaze
- 1. Put milk chocolate in medium bowl. In small saucepan heat cream to a gentle boil. Pour hot cream over chocolate. Let mixture stand for 30 seconds. Whisk until smooth. Stir in vanilla. Cool glaze until it starts to thicken slightly.
- 2. Place cake on a wire rack over baking sheet. Pour milk chocolate glaze over cake, covering it completely. Refrigerate on wire rack for 5 minutes or until glaze is set. Sprinkle cake with chopped peanuts and refrigerate until serving.

132.   Pecan Streusel Topped Pumpkin Cranberry Muffins Recipe

Serving: 35 | Prep: | Cook: 28mins | Ready in:

Ingredients

- FOR THE MUFFINS:
- 15 ounce can of pumpkin
- 4 eggs, beaten
- 1 cup vegetable oil
- 2/3 cup water
- 3 cups sugar
- 3 & 1/2 cups all purpose flour
- 2 teaspoons baking soda
- 1 & 1/2 teaspoons salt

- 1 & 1/2 teaspoons each: cinnamon and nutmeg
- 3/4 teaspoon ground cloves
- 1/2 teaspoon ground ginger
- 3/4 cup (total) mix of dried cranberries and fresh ones (add more if you wish)
- pecan STREUSEL TOPPING:
- 6 ounce bag of pecans that you have ground or chopped
- 9 tablespoons brown sugar
- 5 tablespoons whole wheat pastry flour (can use regular whole wheat too)
- 4 tablespoons oatmeal (uncooked)
- 1 stick of unsalted butter
- (sorry about odd measurements-this recipe covers 35 muffins with a smidge left over for future use-can freeze it)

Direction

- Preheat oven to 350°. Lightly grease muffin tins or use cupcake papers. Grease loaf pans if you wish to bake it into small 7x3 loaves (makes 3)
- FOR THE MUFFINS:
- Mix together the spices with sugar, baking soda, salt.
- Add spice mix to flour and stir so it's mixed well.
- Mix together pumpkin, water, eggs and oil.
- Add pumpkin mix to flour mix and mix well.
- Gently stir in fruit.
- Pour batter into prepared pan. Top with Streusel mix. Bake for about 28 minutes (for muffins) until tester comes out clean. For the loaves it may take a little longer to bake-but use the same standard "until tester comes out clean".
- FOR THE STREUSEL MIX:
- Melt butter.
- Mix all other ingredients together well, then drizzle with melted butter and mix well. Top the muffins/loaves with this mix.

133. Pineapple Coconut And Carrot Cupcakes Recipe

Serving: 12 | Prep: | Cook: 25mins | Ready in:

Ingredients

- 1/2 cup chopped walnut
- 2 cups flour
- 2 tsp. baking soda
- ½ tsp. salt
- 2 tsp. ground cinnamon
- 3 large eggs
- 1 1/2 cup sugar
- 3/4 cup buttermilk
- 1/2 cup oil
- 1 tsp. vanilla extract
- 1 20 ounce can crushed pineapple, drianed, juice reserved
- 1 1/2 cup grated carrots
- 1 cup flaked coconut (for rispy and crunchy flanes, bake on cookies sheet for 8 minutes)
- frosting
- 2 tabespoons flaked coconut
- 12 ounes cream cheese
- ½ cup cofectioners' sugar, sifted dish
- 1 ½ tsp. vanilla extract

Direction

- Preheat oven to 350 F. Toast walnuts in a small baking pan in the oven until fragrant, 10 minutes
- Sift and mix dry ingredients in a large bowl.
- Blend liquid ingredients in another bowl…
- Pour liquid ingredients into dry ingredients and mix well…
- Add pineapple, coconut, carrots and walnuts. Mix with a rubber spatula just until blended, stir in the nuts. Scrape the batter into cupcakes… spreading evenly.
- Bake cupcakes until the top springs back when touched lightly and toothpick inserted in the centre comes out clean, 40 to 45 minutes. Let cool completely.
- Frosting

- Place coconut in a small baking pan and toast in the oven at 300 F, until Light golden.
- Beat cream cheese, confectioners' sugar and vanilla in a mixing bowl with an electric mixer until smooth and creamy. Spread frosting over cooled cupcakes.
- Enjoy

134. Pink Peppermint Cupcakes Recipe

Serving: 30 | Prep: | Cook: 20mins | Ready in:

Ingredients

- 1 pkg (18 1/4 oz) white cake mix
- 1 1/3 cups water
- 3 egg whites
- 2 tblpns veg oil or melted butter
- 1/2 tsp peppermint extract
- 3 to 4 drops red food coloring
- 1 container (16 oz) prepared vanilla frosting
- 1/2 cup crushed peppermint candies (about 16 candies)

Direction

- Pre-heat oven to 350 degrees
- Line 30 standard (2 1/2") muffin pan cups with pink or white baking paper cups
- Beat cake mix, water, egg whites, oil, peppermint extract & food colouring with mixer on low speed for about 30 seconds. Then beat at medium speed about 2 minutes
- Spoon batter into prepared muffin cups, filling 3/4 full
- Bake 20 to 22 minutes until a tooth pick inserted into the centres comes out clean
- Cool in pans for 10 minutes & then remove cupcakes to wire racks to cool completely
- Spread frosting over cooled cakes & sprinkle with crushed peppermint candies

135. Pink Velvet Cupcakes Recipe

Serving: 24 | Prep: | Cook: 25mins | Ready in:

Ingredients

- 1 cup butter, softened
- 1-1/4 cups sugar
- 1/8 teaspoon pink paste food coloring
- 3 eggs
- 1 teaspoon vanilla extract
- 2-1/2 cups all-purpose flour
- 1-1/2 teaspoons baking powder
- 1/4 teaspoon baking soda
- 1/4 teaspoon salt
- 1 cup buttermilk
- white chocolate GANACHE:
- 2 cups white baking chips
- 1 tablespoon butter
- 1/2 cup heavy whipping cream
- Pink coarse sugar and edible glitter

Direction

- In a large bowl, cream the butter, sugar and food colouring until light and fluffy.
- Add eggs, one at a time, beating well after each addition.
- Beat in vanilla.
- Combine the flour, baking powder, baking soda and salt; add to creamed mixture alternately with buttermilk beating well after each addition.
- Fill paper-lined muffin cups two-thirds full.
- Bake at 350° for 23-27 minutes or until a toothpick inserted near the centre comes out clean.
- Cool for 10 minutes before removing from pans to wire racks to cool completely.
- Meanwhile, in a heavy saucepan, melt chips and butter with cream over low heat; stir until smooth.
- Transfer to a large bowl.
- Chill for 30 minutes, stirring once.
- Beat on high for 2-3 minutes or until soft peaks form and frosting is light and fluffy.

- Cut a small hole in the corner of a pastry or plastic bag; insert #30 star tip.
- Fill bag with frosting; frost cupcakes.
- Sprinkle with coarse sugar and edible glitter.
- Store in the refrigerator.
- Yield: 2 dozen.

136. Pistachio Cupcakes Recipe

Serving: 24 | Prep: | Cook: 22mins | Ready in:

Ingredients

- 1/2c shelled pistachios, toasted
- 1 pkg(18.25oz) classic white cake mix
- 2 eggs
- 1pkg
- 1 (3.4oz) instant pistachio pudding mix
- 6 drops green liquid food coloring, optional
- 1 cont.(15 oz) classic vanilla frosting 1tsp almond extract
- chopped pistachios for garnish

Direction

- Preheat oven to 350. Line 24 muffin cups with liners. In food processor, ring pistachios; reserve.
- On med speed, beat cake mix, 11/3 c water, eggs and pudding mix 2 mins. Stir in nuts and if desired, food colouring. Divide among liners. Bake 20-22 mins. Transfer to racks, cool.
- Mix frosting and extract spread over cupcakes. If desired, garnish with chopped nuts.

137. Plum Chocolate Cupcakes With Chocolate Ganache And Walnut Frosting Recipe

Serving: 18 | Prep: | Cook: 48mins | Ready in:

Ingredients

- CUPCAKES:
- 8 ounce bar 61% cacao chocolate
- 3 sticks unsalted butter, room temperature
- 2 1/4 cups sugar
- 8 eggs, room temperature
- 1 1/4 cups flour
- 1/4 cup unsweetened cocoa powder
- 1 1/2 teaspoons baking powder
- Pinch of salt
- 1/2 pound dried plums (preferable unsulphured) OR apricots
- Bottle of good cognac OR armagnac
- GANACHE with WALNUTS:
- 4 ounces semisweet chocolate
- 5 ounces bittersweet chocolate
- 1 cup heavy whipping cream
- 2 tablespoons unsalted butter, room temperature
- 1 teaspoon vanilla extract
- 2 cups powdered sugar
- Shelled walnuts

Direction

- CUPCAKES:
- Chop the plums OR apricots and place in non-reactive bowl.
- Cover fruit with liquor and let plump overnight.
- Preheat oven to 350 degrees F.
- Melt chocolate and butter over a water bath.
- Add sugar and stir; let sit for about 10 minutes.
- Beat with an electric mixer for 3 minutes.
- Add one egg at a time, mixing for 30 seconds between each addition.
- Sift in dry ingredients.

- Mix until just blended.
- Drain the fruit and lightly pat them dry.
- Fold into batter.
- Scoop into cupcake papers.
- Bake for 20 to 24 minutes OR until toothpick comes out clean.
- GANACHE:
- Chop chocolates and transfer to a heat proof bowl.
- Heat cream in a saucepan until bubbles form around edge of pan.
- Pour cream over chocolate.
- Let sit for 1 minutes and then stir until combined.
- Add butter and vanilla and stir until combined.
- Transfer to bowl of electric mixer and let cool for 10 minutes.
- Sift powdered sugar in and mix until combined.
- Continue to beat until creamy and light in colour.
- Spread OR pipe ganache onto cupcakes.
- Top with walnuts.

138. Pretty In Pink Peppermint Cupcakes Recipe

Serving: 30 | Prep: | Cook: 21mins | Ready in:

Ingredients

- 1 package white cake mix
- 1 1/3 cups water
- 3 large eggs
- 2 tbsp vege. oil
- 1/2 tsp peppermint extract
- 3 to 4 drops red liquid food coloring
- 1 container perpared vanilla frosting
- 1/2 cup crushed peppermint candies(about 16 candies)

Direction

- Preheat oven to 350*.
- Line muffin pan with pink or white paper liners
- Beat cake mix, water, eggs, oil, peppermint extract and food colouring with mixer at low speed for 30 seconds.
- Beat at medium speed for 2 minutes
- Spoon batter into prepared cups filling 3/4 full.
- Bake 20 to 22 minutes.
- Cool in pans for 12 minutes
- Remove cupcakes to racks and cool
- Spread cupcakes with frosting top with crushed candies.

139. Pumpkin Cupcakes With Cream Cheese Frosting Recipe

Serving: 24 | Prep: | Cook: 18mins | Ready in:

Ingredients

- 1 yellow cake mix
- 1/3 cup oil
- 3 eggs
- 1/2 teaspoon pumpkin pie spice
- 1 (15 oz) can pumpkin puree
- 2 (8oz) bars cream cheese, room temperature
- 2 cups confectioner's sugar
- 24 pieces corn candy

Direction

- Heat oven to 350 degrees
- Line two regular sized, 12 cup muffin tins with paper liners
- Mix cake mix, oil, eggs, and use the pumpkin puree instead of the water that is called for on the box
- Divide the batter into the lined tins and bake until a toothpick inserted into the centre of a cupcake comes out clean, or about 18 minutes
- Meanwhile, using an electric mixer, beat the cream cheese and sugar until creamy

- Spread or pipe the icing from a cake icing decorator onto the cooled cupcakes and top with candy corn

140. Pumpkin Cupcakes With Maple Cream Cheese Frosting Recipe

Serving: 24 | Prep: | Cook: 25mins | Ready in:

Ingredients

- Cupcakes:
- 2 1/4 cups flour
- 1 tbls. baking powder
- 1/2 tsp. baking soda
- 1/2 tsp. salt
- 1 tsp. cinnamon
- 1 stick butter, softened
- 1 1/3 cups brown sugar, packed
- 2 eggs
- 1 cup canned pumpkin
- 3/4 cup milk
- 3/4 cup walnuts or pecans, chopped
- frosting
- 1/2 stick butter, softened
- 8 oz. cream cheese, softened
- 3 cups powdered sugar
- 1/2 cup maple syrup
- 2 tsp. vanilla extract

Direction

- Preheat oven to 375
- Line 2 muffin tins with liners
- Sift together flour and next 4 ingredients
- In another mixing bowl, beat butter and brown sugar until light and fluffy
- Add eggs, 1 at a time, beating well after adding each egg
- Add pumpkin, beating on low until combined
- Add flour mixture and milk alternately to sugar mixture, beginning and ending with flour until combined
- Stir in nuts
- Spoon batter into muffin cups, filling each about 2/3 full
- Bake 25 minutes or so
- Cool on baking rack
- Frosting
- In large mixing bowl, add all ingredients and beat until smooth
- Spread icing onto top of cooled cupcakes

141. Pumpkin Ginger Cupcakes

Serving: 0 | Prep: | Cook: | Ready in:

Ingredients

- 2 cups all-purpose flour
- 1 (3.4 ounce) package instant butterscotch pudding mix
- 2 teaspoons baking soda
- ¼ teaspoon salt
- 1 tablespoon ground cinnamon
- ½ teaspoon ground ginger
- ½ teaspoon ground allspice
- ¼ teaspoon ground cloves
- ⅓ cup finely chopped crystallized ginger
- 1 cup butter, room temperature
- 1 cup white sugar
- 1 cup packed brown sugar
- 4 large eggs eggs, room temperature
- 1 teaspoon vanilla extract
- 1 (15 ounce) can pumpkin puree

Direction

- Preheat an oven to 350 degrees F (175 degrees C). Grease 24 muffin cups, or line with paper muffin liners. Whisk together the flour, pudding mix, baking soda, salt, cinnamon, ground ginger, allspice, cloves, and crystallized ginger in a bowl; set aside.
- Beat the butter, white sugar, and brown sugar with an electric mixer in a large bowl until

light and fluffy. The mixture should be noticeably lighter in color. Add the eggs one at a time, allowing each egg to blend into the butter mixture before adding the next. Beat in the vanilla and pumpkin puree with the last egg. Stir in the flour mixture, mixing until just incorporated. Pour the batter into the prepared muffin cups.
- Bake in the preheated oven until golden and the tops spring back when lightly pressed, about 20 minutes. Cool in the pans for 10 minutes before removing to cool completely on a wire rack.
- Nutrition Facts
- Per Serving:
- 210.6 calories; protein 2.4g 5% DV; carbohydrates 31.8g 10% DV; fat 8.7g 13% DV; cholesterol 51.3mg 17% DV; sodium 303.2mg 12% DV.

142. Rain Drop Cupcakes Recipe

Serving: 12 | Prep: | Cook: 20mins | Ready in:

Ingredients

- 1 package white cake mix
- 1 small package berry blue gelatin
- 1 cup boiling water
- 8 ounce container frozen whipped topping thawed
- Decorating gel or colored sugar

Direction

- Heat oven to 350.
- Prepare cake batter as directed on package using egg whites.
- Spoon batter into paper lined muffin pan filling each cup 1/2 full.
- Bake as directed on package.
- Cool cupcakes in pan 15 minutes then pierce with two pronged meat fork at 1/4" intervals.

- Dissolve gelatine completely in boiling water then gradually spoon over cupcakes.
- Refrigerate 4 hours then frost with whipped topping.
- Draw umbrellas on cupcakes with decorating gel and sprinkle with sugar.

143. Red Velvet Cupakes Recipe

Serving: 18 | Prep: | Cook: 30mins | Ready in:

Ingredients

- For cupcakes:
- 2 1/2 cups cake flour
- 1 1/2 cups sugar
- 1 tsp baking soda
- Pinch of salt
- 3 tsp cocoa powder
- 1 cup vegetable oil
- 1 cup lowfat buttermilk
- 2 large eggs
- 4 tbs red dye
- 1 tsp white vinegar
- For frosting:
- 8oz cream cheese
- 1 stick butter
- 1 cup powdered sugar
- 2 tsp vanilla
- maraschino cherries
- Red sprinkles

Direction

- Sift together the cake flour, sugar, baking soda, salt, and cocoa power in a bowl and set aside. In another bowl mix the wet ingredients; vegetable oil, buttermilk, vinegar, eggs, and red food colouring. Once the wet ingredients are mixed well mix in the dry ingredients a little at a bit, folding the wet ingredients over them until both bowls have been mixed together. Place in the oven at 350. I made these cupcakes quite large so they took 30 minutes,

if you make smaller cupcakes then you will have to wait less time, around 20-22 minutes.
- For the frosting you beat together the cream cheese and butter until smooth and then slowly mix in the powdered sugar. You can use more powdered sugar if desired but I prefer my frosting to not be super sweet. Cut maraschino cherries in half and put them on top, add a dash of sprinkles. Voila!

144. Red Velvet Cupcakes For Two Recipe

Serving: 2 | Prep: | Cook: 15mins | Ready in:

Ingredients

- Cupcakes
- 1/3 plus 1 tbsp AP flour
- 1/8 baking soda
- 1/8 tsp salt
- 2 tsp unsweetened Dutch processed cocoa powder
- 1/4 cup canola oil
- 1/4 cup sugar
- 2 tbsp buttermilk
- 1 large egg white
- 1 tsp red food coloring
- 1/8 tsp white vinegar
- 1/4 tsp vanilla extract
- frosting
- 3 oz cream cheese, softened
- 2 tbsp butter, softened
- 6 tbsp confectioners sugar, sifted
- 1 tsp milk
- 1/4 tsp vanilla extract
- 1 drop red food coloring

Direction

- Preheat oven to 350F. Line 4 cups of muffin tin with liners, outside edges will rise higher.
- Cupcakes
- Combine flour, baking soda, salt and cocoa powder in a mixing bowl.
- In a separate bowl, beat together oil, sugar, buttermilk, egg, colouring, vinegar and vanilla.
- Slowly add dry ingredients into wet, mixing as you go.
- Divide batter between four cupcake liners. Bake for 20-22 minutes until a toothpick comes out clean.
- Let cool completely on a wire rack.
- Frosting
- Combine all ingredients in a mixing bowl and beat together until well incorporated. Frost cupcakes. I piped my icing out of a plastic sandwich bag with a small corner cut out.

145. Red Velvet Cupcakes Recipe

Serving: 12 | Prep: | Cook: 25mins | Ready in:

Ingredients

- Cake:
- 2 1/4 cups all-purpose flour
- 1 1/2 teaspoons baking soda
- Pinch salt
- 1 cup buttermilk
- 1 tablespoon white vinegar
- 1 teaspoon vanilla extract
- 2 large eggs
- 2 tablespoons natural cocoa powder
- 2 tablespoons red food coloring
- 12 tablespoons unsalted butter, softened
- 1 1/2 cups granulated sugar
- Frosting:
- 16 tablespoons unsalted butter, softened
- 4 cups confectioners' sugar
- 16 ounces cream cheese, cut into 8 pieces, softened
- 1 1/2 teaspoons vanilla extract
- Pinch salt

Direction

- For the cake: Adjust oven rack to middle position and heat oven to 350 degrees. Grease and flour two 9-inch cake pans. Whisk flour, baking soda, and salt in medium bowl. Whisk buttermilk, vinegar, vanilla, and eggs in large measuring cup. Mix cocoa with food colouring in small bowl until a smooth paste forms.
- With electric mixer on medium-high speed, beat butter and sugar together until fluffy, about 2 minutes, scraping down bowl as necessary. Add one-third of flour mixture and beat on medium-low speed until just incorporated, about 30 seconds. Add half of buttermilk mixture and beat on low speed until combined, about 30 seconds. Scrape down bowl as necessary and repeat with half of remaining flour mixture, remaining buttermilk mixture, and finally remaining flour mixture. Scrape down bowl, add cocoa mixture, and beat on medium speed until completely incorporated, about 30 seconds. Using rubber spatula, give batter final stir.
- Scrape into prepared pans and bake until toothpick inserted in centre comes out clean, about 25 minutes. Cool cakes in pans 10 minutes then turn out onto rack to cool completely, at least 30 minutes.
- For the frosting: With electric mixer, beat butter and sugar on medium-high speed until fluffy, about 2 minutes. Add cream cheese, one piece at a time, and beat until incorporated, about 30 seconds. Beat in vanilla and salt. Refrigerate until ready to use.
- When cakes are cooled, spread about 2 cups frosting on one cake layer. Top with second cake layer and spread top and sides of cake with remaining frosting. Cover and refrigerate until ready to serve, up to 3 days.

146. Red Velvet Cupcakes With Cream Cheese Frosting Recipe

Serving: 12 | Prep: | Cook: 25mins | Ready in:

Ingredients

- For the cupcakes:
- 2 1/2 cups all-purpose flour
- 1 1/2 cups sugar
- 1 teaspoon baking soda
- 1 teaspoon salt
- 1 teaspoon cocoa powder
- 1 1/2 cups vegetable oil
- 1 cup buttermilk, room temperature
- 2 large eggs, room temperature
- 2 tablespoons red food coloring
- 1 teaspoon white distilled vinegar
- 1 teaspoon vanilla extract
- For the Cream Cheese Frosting:
- 1 pound cream cheese, softened
- 2 sticks butter, softened
- 1 teaspoon vanilla extract
- 4 cups sifted confectioners' sugar
- Chopped pecans and fresh raspberries or strawberries, for garnish

Direction

- For the cupcakes:
- Preheat the oven to 350 degrees F. Line 2 (12-cup) muffin pans with cupcake papers.
- In a medium mixing bowl, sift together the flour, sugar, baking soda, salt, and cocoa powder.
- In a large bowl gently beat together the oil, buttermilk, eggs, food colouring, vinegar, and vanilla with a handheld electric mixer.
- Add the sifted dry ingredients to the wet and mix until smooth and thoroughly combined.
- Divide the batter evenly among the cupcake tins about 2/3 filled.
- Bake in oven for about 20 to 22 minutes, turning the pans once, half way through. Test the cupcakes with a toothpick for doneness.
- Remove from oven and cool completely before frosting.
- For the Cream Cheese Frosting:
- In a large mixing bowl, beat the cream cheese, butter and vanilla together until smooth.

- Add the sugar and on low speed, beat until incorporated. Increase the speed to high and mix until very light and fluffy.
- Garnish with chopped pecans and a fresh raspberry or strawberry.

147. Red Velvet Puffs With Espresso Frosting Recipe

Serving: 24 | Prep: | Cook: 15mins | Ready in:

Ingredients

- 2 3/4 oz soft tofu
- 1/2 tbsp vanilla extract
- 1/4 cup sugar
- 1/4 cup Splenda granular
- 2 tbsp shortening
- 2 tbsp apple butter
- 1 1/2 tbsp cocoa
- 1 1/2 tbsp red food colouring
- 2 tbsp hot water
- 3/4 cup flour
- 1/2 cup whole-wheat flour
- 1/3 cup low-fat sour cream
- 4 tbsp 1% milk
- 1/2 tbsp cider vinegar
- 1 tsp baking soda
- 2 oz soft tofu
- 2 tbsp fat-free cream cheese
- 1 oz butter, softened
- 1 tsp instant espresso powder (or to taste)
- 3 tbsp powdered sugar
- 1 tbsp raw sugar

Direction

- Preheat oven to 350F, grease 24 mini-muffin cups.
- Puree tofu and vanilla extract, set aside.
- Cream sugar, Splenda, shortening and apple butter.
- Add tofu puree and blend well.
- Make a paste of the cocoa, food colouring, and hot water, add to above mixture.
- Combine flours in another small bowl, as well as combining sour cream and milk in yet another bowl.
- Add flour and sour cream mixtures, alternating, to form a smooth batter.
- Combine vinegar and baking soda, quickly fold into batter.
- Portion cupcakes into prepared tins.
- Bake 15 minutes and turn out immediately onto wire racks to cool completely.
- In a food processor or blender, puree tofu, cream cheese, butter, espresso powder and powdered sugar until smooth and fluffy.
- Ice cupcakes, and decorate each with a sprinkle of the raw sugar.
- Keep in the refrigerator until serving.

148. Rich Double Chocolate Zucchini Muffins Recipe

Serving: 26 | Prep: | Cook: 28mins | Ready in:

Ingredients

- 2 cups flour
- 1 cup whole wheat flour
- 1 tsp baking soda
- 1 tsp baking powder
- 1 tsp salt
- 1/4 cup Nestle Quik chocolate drink mix powder
- 1/3 cup unsweetened cocoa
- 1/2 cup melted butter
- 1 oz unsweetened chocolate, melted
- 1/4 cup brown sugar
- 1 cup sugar
- 1 cup low-fat vanilla yogurt
- 2 eggs
- 3 medium zucchini, shredded
- 1/2 cup white chocolate chips

Direction

- Preheat oven to 350F, grease and line muffin tin.
- In a medium bowl, whisk together flours, baking soda, baking powder, salt, Nesquik and cocoa. Set aside.
- In a large bowl, combine butter, chocolate, sugars, yogurt, eggs and zucchini, mixing well.
- Add the dry ingredients and mix until blended.
- Fold in the chocolate chips.
- Bake for 20-25 minutes, until they test done.

149. Rocky Road Cupcakes Recipe

Serving: 24 | Prep: | Cook: 22mins | Ready in:

Ingredients

- 1 box (1 lb. 2.25 oz.) devil's food cake mix
- 1 1/2 C miniature marshmallows
- 1 C Mini semisweet chocolate chips
- 1/2 C chopped pecans or walnuts

Direction

- Heat oven to 350 degrees.
- Line 24 muffin cups with paper or foil liners.
- Prepare batter as box directs.
- Add remaining ingredients; stir until well blended.
- Spoon into lined cups.
- Bake 20 to 22 minutes until a wooden pick inserted in centre of cupcakes comes out clean.
- Cool in pan on a wire rack 5 minutes before removing from pan to wire rack to cool completely.

150. Root Beer Cup Cakes Recipe

Serving: 24 | Prep: | Cook: 20mins | Ready in:

Ingredients

- 2 1/2 cups old-fashioned style root beer (like A&W or Dads)
- ~~~~You will need a little more root beer for the top of the cupcakes later
- 2 tsp. vanilla extract
- 2 cups dark brown sugar
- 1 cup butter
- 2 eggs
- 3 cups all purpose flour
- 1 TBL. baking powder
- 2 tsp. baking soda
- 1 tsp. salt
- ~~~~~~root beer Glaze~~~~~~
- 2 cups confectioners sugar
- 1/3 cup root beer (more or less)
- Whip together till smooth
- ~~~~~buttercream Frosting~~~~~~
- 1 cup confectioners sugar
- 2 TBL butter (softened)
- 2 tsp vanilla
- Whip together till smooth

Direction

- Preheat oven to 350°F.
- In a bowl, mix together root beer and vanilla. Set aside.
- In a separate bowl, combine flour, baking soda, baking powder and salt. Set Aside
- In a separate mixing bowl, cream together butter and sugar until light and fluffy.
- Add eggs to butter sugar mixture, mix until smooth
- Mix with mixer on lowest speed, s l o w l y pour in root beer mixture.
- Mix until smooth and lump free. Stir frequently with spatula.
- Pour into lined cupcake pan. (Use foil cupcake liners to avoid "leakage" later.) Fill nearly to the top, you may think it's over-filled, but it

- puffs up perfectly this way. Do not be tempted to use more than 24 cupcake cups!
- Bake for 15- 20 minutes, until golden brown and cake springs back when touched.
- While cupcakes are baking, prepare butter cream frosting and root beer glaze in separate bowls.
- When cupcakes are done, let them cool for about 10 minutes.
- While still slightly warm, pour 1 tsp. root beer over each cupcake. Pour on slowly to allow root beer to soak in.
- Wait about 5minutes to let root beer soak into cupcakes.
- Pour a teaspoon of glaze on each cupcake
- When the glaze sets a bit, about 5 minutes, put a dollop of buttercream frosting atop each cupcake.

151.   Rootbeer Cupcakes With A Butter Cream Glaze Recipe

Serving: 24 | Prep: | Cook: 15mins |Ready in:

Ingredients

- 1 cup root beer schnapps
- 1 1/2 cups old-fashioned style root beer (like A&W or Dads)
- 2 tsp. vanilla extract or root beer if you can find.
- 2 cups dark brown sugar
- 1 cup butter
- 2 eggs
- 3 cups all purpose flour
- 1 Tbs. baking powder
- 2 tsp. baking soda
- 1 tsp. salt
- root beer glaze
- 4 cups confectioners sugar
- 1/3 cup root beer
- 3 Tbs. root beer schnapps*
- 3 Tbs. vegetable oil
- *for a more kid friendly version, replace schnapps with more root beer
- You will also need some extra root beer schnapps (1 Tbs. per cupcake)
- Or for the kiddies use root beer (again 1 Tbs. per cupcake)
- You will also need some basic vanilla buttercream (there are many recipes online to try)
- or buy betty crocker frosting it works well to.

Direction

- PLEASE READ BEFORE BAKING:
- 1. USE LINERS. Use foil liners. And no, do not take the liners off.
- 2. If you can find root beer extract, more power to you, you can replace the vanilla extract with it. .
- 3. The glaze. A) Pour on the glaze while the cupcakes are still slightly warm like I say, it will soak in a bit, and some of the moisture will be taken out of the glaze and into the cupcake... once you let it set up a bit it shouldn't be too sticky. ... I did not add schnapps to the buttercream as that's the "vanilla float" part. .you can also use whipped cream this is yummy to
- 4. I say to fill the liners to the top with the batter, that works for my oven, they puff perfectly. But, I forgot my Alton Brown, and every oven is different... so filling to the top may not work for you... so if you are worried... don't do it, but you will end up with a few more cupcakes.
- 1. Preheat oven to 350ºF.
- 2. In a bowl, mix together root beer schnapps, root beer, and vanilla extract. Set aside.
- 3. In a separate bowl, cream together butter and sugar until light and fluffy.
- 4. Add eggs, mix until smooth
- 5. Sift in flour, baking soda, baking powder and salt.
- 6. Mix with hand mixer on low, while slowly pouring in root beer mixture.
- 7. Mix until smooth and lump free.

- 8. Pour into lined cupcake pan. (Use foil cupcake liners to avoid "leakage" later.) Fill nearly to the top, you may think it's over-filled, but it puffs up perfectly this way. Don't be tempted to use more than 24 cupcake cups... trust me.
- 9. Bake for 15- 20 minutes, until golden brown and cake springs back when touched.
- 10. While cupcakes are baking, prepare your butter cream and root beer glaze. For glaze, put all ingredients into a bowl and mix with a whisk until smooth and lump free.
- 11. To assemble, start by letting cupcakes cool, still in the pan.
- 12. While still slightly warm, pour 1 Tbs. of root beer schnapps over each cupcake. Pour on slowly to allow schnapps (or regular root beer for the kiddies) to soak in.
- 13. Once the schnapps has soaked in and let sit for a few minutes, pour a couple tablespoons of glaze over each cupcake.
- 14. When the glaze sets up a bit and isn't too runny, put a "scoop" of buttercream atop each. For an added touch, you can even place a root beer barrel candy on each one.

152. Rootbeer Float Cupcakes Recipe

Serving: 12 | Prep: | Cook: 20mins | Ready in:

Ingredients

- Cupcake:
- 1 Cup Rootbeer Soda
- 1 Teaspoon apple cider vinegar
- 3/4 Cup sugar
- 1/3 Cup canola oil
- 1/2 Teaspoon vanilla extract
- 2 Teaspoons Rootbeer extract
- 1 1/3 Cups flour
- 3/4 Teaspoon baking soda
- 1/2 Teaspoon baking powder
- Pinch of salt
- Ganache:
- 5 Oz. dark chocolate
- 1/4 Cup soymilk
- 1 Tablespoon maple syrup
- Frosting:
- 1 Cup vegetable shortening
- 3 Cups Confectioner's sugar
- 2 Tablespoons vanilla soymilk
- 2 Teaspoons vanilla extract

Direction

- Preheat your oven to 350 degrees and line a dozen cupcake tins with papers.
- Combine the soda and vinegar and let stand for a few minutes. Add in the sugar and oil, whisking vigorously until slightly frothy. Integrate your extracts, and gently introduce the flour, along with the baking powder / soda, and salt, being careful not to over mix.
- Distributing the batter evenly between the prepared tins, fill cupcake liners approximately 3/4 of the way to the top. Bake for about 18 - 22 minutes. Allow them to cool completely before proceeding to the ganache.
- Combine all of the ingredients for the ganache in a microwave-safe container and nuke for about a minute. Stir thoroughly even if it doesn't look completely melted - It should come together after a bit of agitation, but if the chocolate still isn't entirely smooth, return to the microwave for 15-30 seconds at a time, watching carefully to ensure that it doesn't burn. Drizzle ganache in squiggles over the tops of the cupcakes. [You'll probably have plenty of left over ganache, but is that a particularly bad thing?] Allow ganache squiggles to fully cool and dry before preparing the frosting.
- Finally, for the frosting, throw room temperature shortening into your mixer, and beat thoroughly until creamed. Add in sugar and start on a low speed so as not to spray powder everywhere. Incorporate soymilk and extract, and combine thoroughly. Apply to cupcakes as desired. Wax nostalgic about childhood memories.

153. STRAWBERRY CUPCAKES WITH STRAWBERRY WHIPPED CREAM FROSTING Recipe

Serving: 24 | Prep: | Cook: 22mins | Ready in:

Ingredients

- strawberry sauce for cupcakes:
- 2 cups of fresh strawberries, cut in half and stem removed
- sugar to taste
- cupcakes:
- 1/2 cup (1 stick) unsalted butter, room temperature
- 1 cup sugar
- 2 large eggs, room temperature
- 1-1/3 cups all-purpose flour
- 1/2 teaspoon baking powder
- 1/2 teaspoon baking soda
- 1/8 teaspoon salt
- 1/2 cup strawberry sauce
- 1/4 cup milk
- frosting:
- 1 packet unflavored gelatin, sprinkled into 4 tsp cold water left to sit for a few minutes, then heated until dissolved.
- 1 container lowfat strawberry yogurt
- same amount of heavy whipping cream
- a tablespoonful or so of sugar

Direction

- Strawberry sauce for cupcakes: Macerate strawberries with about 1-2 tbsp. sugar for 15 minutes. Put strawberries in a small saucepan and heat under medium heat with lid on. Cook strawberries for approximately 15 minutes till strawberries cook down and become soft and saucy. Adjust sweetness with sugar until you get the desired sweetness. Using a hand blender, puree until you get the desired smoothness or chunkiness. Cool before using in recipe.
- Cupcakes: Beat butter on high until soft, about 30 seconds. Add sugar. Beat on medium-high until light and fluffy, about 3 minutes. Add eggs one at a time, beat for 30 seconds between each. Whisk together flour, baking powder, baking soda, and salt in a bowl. Measure out milk and strawberry sauce together. Add about a fourth of the flour to the butter/sugar mixture and beat to combine. Add about one third the milk/strawberry sauce mixture and beat until combined. Repeat above, alternating flour and milk and ending with the flour mixture. Scoop into cupcake papers about half to three-quarters full (depending on whether you want flat or domed cupcakes). Bake for 20-22 minutes at 350F until a cake tester comes out clean.
- Frosting:
- Whip these ingredients together until thickened but not stiff with an electric mixer. Put the mixer on 'high' then slowly drizzle the melted gelatine into the yogurt mix until well incorporated.
- Transfer into one of those Ziploc type storage bags and refrigerate. It will set in about ten minutes. Cut a small corner off of one end of the bag and squeeze the whipped yogurt onto the top of a cooled cupcake.

154. Skinny Hummingbird Cupcakes Recipe

Serving: 22 | Prep: | Cook: 25mins | Ready in:

Ingredients

- Servings: 22 • Serving Size: 1 cupcake • Old Points: 4 pts • Points+: 5 pts
- Calories: 197.8 • Fat: 6.5 g • Protein: 3.0 g • Carb: 31.1 g • Fiber: 1.7 g • Sugar: 21.7 g
- Sodium: 284.2 mg
- Ingredients:

- 3/4 cup all-purpose flour
- 3/4 cup whole wheat flour
- 1 cup sugar (I used raw)
- 2 tsp baking soda
- 1 tsp salt
- 1 tsp ground cinnamon
- 1/4 tsp nutmeg
- 1/4 tsp ground ginger
- 2 tbsp oil
- 2 large eggs
- 1 tsp vanilla
- 2 cups mashed ripe bananas
- 20 oz can crushed pineapple in juice, drained well
- 1/2 cup chopped pecans
- For the Frosting:
- 8 oz 1/3-less fat Philadelphia cream cheese
- 1 cup powdered sugar
- 2 tsp vanilla extract
- 22 pecan halves

Direction

- Directions:
- To prepare frosting, beat together cream cheese, powdered sugar and vanilla until smooth. Refrigerate until ready to use.
- Preheat oven to 350°. In a large bowl, combine flour, sugar, baking soda, salt, and spices; stir well with a whisk.
- In a medium bowl, combine oil, eggs, and vanilla; stir well. Add banana and pineapple; mix well. Fold wet ingredients and chopped pecans with the dry ingredients, batter will be stiff and dry but keep folding it and it will all come together.
- Spoon batter into cupcake tin. Bake at 350° for about 23 minutes, or until a wooden toothpick inserted in the centre comes out clean. Cool completely on a wire rack.
- Spread frosting over the cupcakes once they are cooled. Garnish each cupcake with a pecan half on top.

155. Snickerdoodle Cupcakes Recipe

Serving: 12 | Prep: | Cook: 25mins | Ready in:

Ingredients

- 1 package plain white cake mix
- 1 cup whole milk
- 1 stick of butter, melted
- 3 large eggs
- 1 teaspoon vanilla extract
- 2 teaspoons ground cinnamon
- FROSTING:
- 1 stick butter
- 3 3/4 cup confectioners sugar
- 3-4 Tablespoons milk
- 1 teaspoon vanilla extract
- 1 Tablespoon ground cinnamon

Direction

- Preheat oven to 350 degrees and flour & grease 2 9" pans (for cakes) or line your cupcake tin.
- Place cake mix, milk, melted butter, eggs, vanilla, and cinnamon in a large mixing bowl.
- Blend for three minutes (stop to scrape once).
- Pour into pans and bake for 27-29 minutes (for cake) or 22-25 minutes (for cupcakes).
- Allow the cakes to cool completely.
- Beat butter until fluffy for frosting. Add all other ingredients.
- Note: These freeze very nicely!

156. Snowball Cupcakes Recipe

Serving: 24 | Prep: | Cook: 105mins | Ready in:

Ingredients

- 2c Baker's flaked coconut
- 1/2c sweetened condensed milk

- 1 pkg. Betty Crocker Super-Moist yellow cake mix
- 1 1/4c water
- 1/3c vegetable oil
- 3 eggs
- 1 tub Betty Crocker Rich and Creamy vanilla frosting
- 1c Baker's flaked coconut toasted

Direction

- Heat oven to 350. Place paper baking cup in each of 24 regular size muffin cups
- In med. bowl, stir 2c coconut with condensed milk and set aside.
- In large bowl, beat cake mix, water, oil and eggs with electric mixer on low 30 seconds. Beat on medium for 2 mins, scraping bowl occasionally. Divide batter evenly among muffin cups (3/4 full). Top each with about 1 heaping tsp. coconut mixture. Bake as directed on box for cupcakes. Cool 5 mins; remove from pan to wire rack. Cool completely about 30 mins.
- Frost cupcakes. Dip tops in toasted coconut. Store loosely covered at room temp.

157. Spiced Up Cupppycakes With Cream Cheese Frosting Recipe

Serving: 12 | Prep: | Cook: 17mins | Ready in:

Ingredients

- 1-1/4 cups all-purpose flour
- 1 tsp. baking soda
- 1 tsp. cinnamon
- 1/2 tsp. nutmeg, freshly grated or pre-grated
- 1/4 tsp. ground cloves
- Pinch salt
- 1/4 cup vegetable shortening
- 1/4 cup granulated sugar
- 1 large egg

- 1/2 cup unsulfured molasses stirred together with 1/2 cup boiling water
- 4 ounces cream cheese, softened
- 2 Tbsp. unsalted butter, softened
- 1/2 cup confectioners' sugar

Direction

- Preheat oven to 350 degrees F.
- In a bowl, whisk together flour, baking soda, spices, and a pinch of salt.
- In another bowl, with an electric mixer cream together shortening and granulated sugar, beat in egg, and beat in flour mixture alternately with the molasses mixture, beating well after each addition.
- Divide the batter among 12 paper-lined 1/2-cup muffin tins and bake the cupcakes in the middle of an oven for 15 to 20 minutes, or until a tester comes out clean. Turn the cupcakes out onto a rack and let them cool completely.
- In another bowl, beat together cream cheese, butter, and confectioners' sugar until the icing is fluffy. Spread the icing on the cupcakes and enjoy!

158. Strawberry Cupcakes Recipe

Serving: 24 | Prep: | Cook: 20mins | Ready in:

Ingredients

- 1 box Betty Crocker white cake mix
- 1 cup unsweetened applesauce
- 3/4 cup water
- 3 egg whites
- 1-1/2 cups strawberry yogurt, fat free
- 3/4 cup Lite Cool Whip

Direction

- Heat oven to 350.
- Line 24 cupcake tins with paper wrappers.

- Remove cool whip from freezer to let it thaw.
- Mix together the cake mix, half of the yogurt (only 3/4 cups), the applesauce, the water, and the egg whites.
- Beat on medium speed until tasty-looking (i.e., smooth).
- Pour into 24 prepared cupcake tins lined with paper wrappers. Each tin should be about 3/4 full.
- Bake for 20-26 minutes, or until a toothpick inserted in the centre comes out clean. Remove and let cool.
- Mix together the cool whip and the remaining 3/4 cup of strawberry yogurt. Spread on cooled cupcakes.
- Serve with sliced strawberries if desired!

159. Strawberry Stuffed Lime Cupcakes Recipe

Serving: 6 | Prep: | Cook: 30mins | Ready in:

Ingredients

- 1 1/2 cups all-purpose flour
- 1 1/2 teaspoons baking powder
- 1/4 teaspoon fine salt
- 2 large eggs, room temperature
- 2/3 cup sugar
- 3/4 cup unsalted butter, melted
- 2 teaspoons pure vanilla extract
- 1/2 cup milk
- 1 1/3 cups confectioners' sugar, sifted
- 1 1/2 tablespoons finely grated lime zest
- 2 tablespoons freshly squeezed lime juice
- 1 drop green food coloring
- 6 large ripe strawberries, hulled
- Green sanding sugar
- fresh mint leaves or candied leaves

Direction

- Preheat the oven to 350 degrees F. Line the muffin tin with cupcake liners.
- Whisk the flour, baking powder, and salt together in a medium bowl.
- In another medium bowl, beat the eggs and sugar with an electric mixer until light and foamy, about 2 minutes. While beating, gradually pour in the butter and then the vanilla.
- While mixing slowly, add half the dry ingredients, then add all the milk, and follow with the rest of the dry ingredients. Take care not to over mix the batter. Divide the batter evenly in the prepared tin.
- Bake until a tester inserted in the centre of the cakes comes out clean, about 30 minutes. Cool cupcakes on a rack in the tin for 10 minutes, then remove. Cool on the rack completely.
- For icing: Mix the confectioners' sugar and lime zest in a medium bowl. Add the lime juice and mix with an electric mixer to make a firm but pourable icing. (If needed, add up to 1 teaspoon more juice, but take care if the icing is too loose it doesn't set properly.) Add food colour to make a pale pastel green icing.
- To assemble: Remove cupcake from its liner. Cut and remove a strawberry (coned) shaped portion of cupcake from the top of each cupcake, leaving about 1/2 to 1-inch of cake in the bottom. Stuff each cake with a strawberry and cover with a little bit of cake. Spoon and spread icing over the top of the cupcakes. Sprinkle with green sanding sugar. Top with small mint leaves or candied leaves.

160. Strawberry Tuxedo Cupcakes Recipe

Serving: 60 | Prep: | Cook: 15mins | Ready in:

Ingredients

- 1 box of red velvet cake mix
- 1 1/4 cups of mixed berry juice (made from frozen concentrate)
- 1/3 cup of cocoa powder

- 1 1/2 tbsp of red food coloring
- 4 eggs
- 1/3 cup of oil
- 60 strawberries, stems on, washed and dried
- 1 bag white chocolate chips
- 1 bag of Ghiradelli semisweet chocolate chips
- 2 tsp of vegetable oil
- mini cup cake liners
- 1 tube of red frosting
- plastic coupler and small round tip
- large can of whipped vanilla frosting-extra fluffy
- 1/2 tsp of almond extract

Direction

- Preheat oven to 350 degrees.
- Place liners in 60 mini muffin tins-5 pans.
- Prepare cake mix as directed, using mixed berry juice instead of water, adding the extra cocoa, eggs, red food colouring and oil.
- Fill cupcake pans only three quarters full.
- You don't want high rounded tops on these little cupcakes,
- You want them flat so that the strawberries will sit on them.
- Bake 13 to 14 minutes.
- Cool on wire racks.
- Whip the canned frosting adding the almond extract. Set aside.
- Prepare two double boilers with simmering water, melt chips separately in each bowl.
- Add a tsp. of oil to each bag of melting chips, stir well.
- Dip the front face of each strawberry in the melted white cocoa chips.
- Set on wax paper lined cookie sheet.
- Chill strawberries until the white chocolate sets.
- Dip each chilled strawberry diagonally in the dark chocolate from each side to just cover the white part leaving a white triangle centre and dark chocolate corners.
- Place on wax paper lined cookie sheet, chill until chocolate sets.
- Using small round tip on the purchased red frosting tube, pipe little dots and one "x" as the bow tie on each strawberry.
- (This is very hard to do with minor arthritic hands, by the way)
- Frost each cupcake with enough of the frosting to make a base for the strawberry and kind of glue it into place.
- Add the strawberry topper to each cup cake.
- Transport is difficult, it can be done with a white shirt box lined with foil and twisted plastic wrap in coils around the outer side of the box to keep the berries from toppling.
- Hope you win the silly contest because it is very late.

161. Strawberry Twinkie Desert Recipe

Serving: 8 | Prep: | Cook: | Ready in:

Ingredients

- 4 cups strawberries, sliced
- 1 (13 1/2 ounce) container strawberry glaze
- 8 twinkies
- 1 (8 ounce) package cream cheese, softened
- 1 (14 ounce) can sweetened condensed milk
- 1 (12 ounce) container whipped topping

Direction

- Combine strawberries and glaze in a small bowl. Slice Twinkies in
- Half lengthwise and place in a single layer over the bottom of a
- 13x9" baking dish.
- In a mixing bowl, beat cream cheese and condensed milk until smooth.
- Fold in whipped topping and spread mixture over Twinkies. Spoon berries over cream cheese mixture. Cover and chill 30 minutes or more. Refrigerate leftovers.

162. Strawberry Cream Cheese Cupcakes Recipe

Serving: 24 | Prep: | Cook: 18mins | Ready in:

Ingredients

- 1 box supermoist yellow cake mix
- 1 container (8 oz.) sour cream
- 1/2 cup vegetable oil
- 1/2 cup water
- 2 eggs
- 3 tablespoons strawberry preserves
- 1 package cream cheese, cut into 24 pieces
- 1 container of rich & creamy cream cheese frosting
- Sliced fresh small strawberries, if desired

Direction

- Heat oven to 350F.
- Place paper baking cup in each of 24 regular-size muffin cups.
- In large bowl, mix cake mix, sour cream, oil, water, eggs with spoon until well blended (batter will be thick).
- Divide batter evenly among muffin cups. In small bowl, stir strawberry preserves until smooth. Place 1 piece of cream cheese on top of batter in each cupcake; press in slightly. Place ¼ measuring teaspoon of preserves over cream cheese. Bake 18 to 23 minutes or until tops are golden brown and spring back when touched lightly in centre (some preserves may show in tops of cupcakes).
- Cool 10 minutes; remove from pan to wire rack. Cool completely, about 30 minutes. Frost with frosting. Just before serving, garnish each cupcake with strawberry slices. Store covered in refrigerator.

163. Sunshine Cupcakes

Serving: 0 | Prep: | Cook: | Ready in:

Ingredients

- 1 package lemon cake mix (regular size)
- 1 can (16 ounces) vanilla frosting
- Yellow food coloring
- Miniature semisweet chocolate chips, red shoestring licorice and candy corn

Direction

- Prepare cake batter mix according to package directions for cupcakes; cool completely.
- In a small bowl, tint frosting yellow. Frost cupcakes. Press two chocolate chips into each cupcake for eyes. For mouths, cut licorice into 1-in. pieces; bend slightly to curve. Press one licorice piece into each cupcake. Add candy corn around edges of cupcakes.
- Nutrition Facts
- 1 each: 208 calories, 10g fat (3g saturated fat), 26mg cholesterol, 195mg sodium, 29g carbohydrate (20g sugars, 0 fiber), 1g protein.

164. Surprise Cupcake Recipe

Serving: 15 | Prep: | Cook: 15mins | Ready in:

Ingredients

- Prepared chocolate Cupcakes.
- Creamcheese filling:
- 2-8 ounces cream cheese, room temperature
- 1 cup powdered sugar
- 1/2 cup stick butter, room temperature
- 2 teaspoons vanilla extract

Direction

- Mix all ingredients with mixer till creamy.
- Fill pastry or icing tube.
- Insert in cooled chocolate cupcakes.
- Enjoy!

165. Sweet Hearts Recipe

Serving: 16 | Prep: | Cook: 35mins | Ready in:

Ingredients

- 1 box Triple chocolate fudge cake mix (I was lazy tonight)
- 3 eggs
- 1 tbspn vanilla extract
- 1 cup butter
- 2 tbspns whole milk (None of that 2% crap!)
- 1/3 cup dark brown sugar
- 1/2 cup confectioner's sugar plus more for topping
- 1 small can Strawberry cake filling
- 2 tbspns honey
- Heart-shaped Reynold's cupcake tins
- Sprinkles or Decorating sugar (Optional)

Direction

- Preheat oven to 350.
- In a large mixing bowl, blend together cake mix, milk, eggs, butter, vanilla and sugars, working the lumps out.
- Put into tins about halfway, batter will be thick.
- Bake for 30-35 minutes or until toothpick inserted into the centre comes out clean.
- Mix together strawberry filling and honey, adding a little confectioner's sugar if desired.
- Remove cupcakes from oven and let cool slightly before smearing the strawberry-honey mixture generously onto the tops.
- Garnish each cupcake with confectioner's sugar, sprinkles and/or decorating sugar if desired.
- They are so yummy, they are bound to get you laid.

166. The Magnolia Bakery Cupcake Recipe Recipe

Serving: 12 | Prep: | Cook: 21mins | Ready in:

Ingredients

- 1 cup (2 sticks) unsalted butter, softened.
- 2 cups sugar
- 4 large eggs, at room temperature
- 1 ½ cup self-rising flour
- 1 ½ cup all-purpose flour
- 1 cup whole milk
- 1 teaspoon vanilla extract

Direction

- 1. Whip butter until very smooth in texture
- 2. Add sugar 1 cup at a time, beating until smooth in texture
- 3. Add eggs, 1 at a time, beating very well between each addition
- 4. In separate bowl, mix the 2 flours together
- 5. In separate bowl, mix Milk and Vanilla
- 6. Add flour mixture and milk mixture 1 cup at a time to Butter mixture. Beating very well between each addition.
- 7. Spoon into lined cupcake pan (approx. ¼ c batter per cupcake)
- 8. Bake for 20-22 minutes in pre heated over (350 degrees F)

167. The Easiest Chocolate Muffins In The World Recipe

Serving: 12 | Prep: | Cook: 25mins | Ready in:

Ingredients

- 1 Package Devil's Food cake mix (I used only half of the batter
- and saved the rest for my next posting)
- 1/3 cup chopped hazelnuts
- 125 g chopped unsweetened chocolate, chopped

- ¾ cup heavy cream
- 2 tbsp butter, softened

Direction

- Preheat oven to 375F. Prepare a 12 muffins tray with paper or silicon cups. Make cake mix as directed on back of package. Fill each muffin cup till 3/4 of the cup. Sprinkle hazelnuts over top of each. Press them slightly with a teaspoon. Bake for 20-25minutes. Cool.
- Glaze:
- Heat the cream until simmering point, pour over the chopped chocolate and stir until smooth. Add the butter and stir until combined. Set aside until thickened slightly and drizzle by tablespoonful over each muffin. Set aside to set for 10 minutes. Using a teaspoon, drizzle the rest of the glaze again in a stripes shape over the top of each muffin. Chill.

168. Tie Die Cupcakes Or Cake Recipe

Serving: 24 | Prep: | Cook: 20mins | Ready in:

Ingredients

- 1 box white cake mix
- wiltons icing colors concetrated paste (at least two)

Direction

- Prepare cake mix as directed.
- Divide into two or three bowls depending on how many different colours you use.
- Add about small amount of paste to the mixes. Add more until you get the desired colour.
- Bake as directed.

169. Tiramisu Cupcakes Recipe

Serving: 18 | Prep: | Cook: 15mins | Ready in:

Ingredients

- Sponge cake
- 1 cup all-purpose flour
- 3/4 teaspoon baking powder
- 1/4 teaspoon salt
- 4 eggs, at room temperature
- 2/3 cup sugar
- 1 1/4 teaspoons vanilla extract
- syrup
- 1/2 cup water
- 1/3 cup sugar
- 2 tablespoons dark rum
- 2 teaspoons instant espresso powder
- Filling
- 8 oz mascarpone
- scant 1/2 cup confectioner's sugar
- 1 tablespoon marsala
- 1/2 cup heavy cream, chilled

Direction

- Preheat the oven to 350 degrees. Line muffin pan with 18 liners. I sprayed the liners with non-stick spray. (I don't know if that's necessary, but the cake didn't stick in the end so it worked)
- In a bowl, whisk together the flour, baking powder, and salt until blended. In a large bowl, using a mixer on medium-high speed, beat the eggs until pale and thick (about 3 min). Add the sugar and vanilla and continue beating until very thick and tripled in volume (about 3 min more). Sprinkle the dry ingredients over the wet ingredients, and using a rubber spatula, fold gently until blended.
- Fill the liners with the batter and baking until a toothpick inserted in the cakes comes out clean. Mine only took around 15 minutes. Let the cake cool completely
- For the syrup:

- Combine the water and the sugar in a small saucepan and cook over medium heat, stirring frequently, until the sugar dissolves. Bring to a boil and remove from the heat. Stir in the rum and espresso powder. Set aside to cool to room temperature.
- Make slits in tops of cupcakes with a sharp knife and then brush on the espresso syrup.
- For the filling:
- Beat together the mascarpone, confectioner's sugar and Marsala in a mixer until well blended. Add the cream for around another 1-2 minutes until it is fluffy.
- Using a pastry bag with the filling mixture, insert the tip in the cupcake to squeeze a small amount. Then frost the tops of the cupcakes with the filling mixture. Sprinkle cocoa powder and chocolate shavings.

170. Toll House Cupcakes Recipe

Serving: 12 | Prep: | Cook: 25mins | Ready in:

Ingredients

- 1/2 c. butter
- 6 tbsp. brown sugar
- 6 tbsp. sugar
- 1/2 tsp. vanilla
- ADD --
- 1 egg
- 1 c. + 2 tbsp. flour
- 1/2 tsp. baking soda
- 1/2 tsp. salt
- Beat above until thick.
- FILLING:--
- 1/2 c. brown sugar
- 1 egg
- 1/8 tsp. salt--
- ADD:--
- 6 oz. semi-sweet chocolate chips
- 1/2 c. chopped walnuts
- 1/2 tsp. vanilla

Direction

- Spoon batter into paper lined tins evenly dividing between 12 cupcakes.
- Bake at 375 degrees for about 10 minutes or until golden. Remove from oven.
- Spoon filling into each cup equally dividing among cupcakes. Bake again for about 15 minutes.

171. Topping 2 For Muffins And Scones Recipe

Serving: 8 | Prep: | Cook: | Ready in:

Ingredients

- 1/2 cup granulated sugar
- 1 teaspoon good quality cinnamon
- 6 tablespoons butter, melted

Direction

- Mix the cinnamon and sugar together in a bowl. When you remove the muffins/scones from the
- Tins, dip the still hot muffins in the butter and then roll the tops in the cinnamon sugar mixture.

172. Tripple Chocolate Muffins Recipe

Serving: 12 | Prep: | Cook: 20mins | Ready in:

Ingredients

- 250 grams/ 9 oz plain flour
- 25 grams/ 1 oz cocoa powder
- 2 tsp baking powder
- ½ tsp bicarbonate of soda
- 85 grams/3 oz each dark,plain and white chocolate, broken

- into chunks
- 2 eggs, beaten
- 284ml carton yogurt
- 85grams sugar
- 85 grams butter, melted
- Filling:
- 175 grams cream cheese
- 5 tbsp powder sugar
- Beat the cheese till creamy then add the sugar and beat till fluffy and
- set aside.

Direction

- Preheat the oven to 400 Butter 12 holes of a muffin tin. In a large bowl, combine the flour, cocoa, baking powder, bicarbonate of soda and chocolate. In a separate bowl, mix together the eggs, yogurt, sugar and butter.
- Add the yogurt mixture to the flour mixture and stir until just combined and the mixture is fairly stiff, but don't overmix. Spoon half the mixture into holes. Insert 1 teaspoon of the cream cheese mixture over each one and then cover with the rest of the chocolate batter.
- Bake for 20 minutes until well risen .Leave in the tins about 15 minutes as the mixture is quite tender. Remove from the tins and cool on a wire rack.
- You may decorate with chocolate ganache rosettes or just serve them plain.

173. Ultimate Chocolate Cupcakes With Ganache Filling Recipe

Serving: 12 | Prep: | Cook: 19mins | Ready in:

Ingredients

- Ganache Filling:
- 2 oz bittersweet chocolate (Callebaut Intense dark chocolate L-60-40NV or Ghirardelli bittersweet chocolate Baking Bar)
- 1/4 cup heavy cream
- 1 tbs confectioners' sugar
- chocolate Cupcake:
- 3 oz bittersweet chocolate (Callebaut Intense dark chocolate L-60-40NV or Ghirardelli bittersweet chocolate Baking Bar)
- 1/3 cup (1oz) Dutch-processed cocoa
- 3/4 cup hot coffee
- 3/4 cup (4 1/8oz) bread flour
- 3/4 cup (5 1/4oz) granulated sugar
- 1/2 tsp table salt
- 1/2 tsp baking soda
- 6 tbs vegetable oil
- 2 large eggs
- 2 tsp white vinegar
- 1 tsp vanilla extract
- Creamy Chocolate Frosting:
- 1/3 cup (2 1/3oz) granulated sugar
- 2 large egg whites
- Pinch table salt
- 12 tbs (1 1/2 sticks) unsalted butter, softened and cut into 1 tbs pieces
- 6 oz bittersweet chocolate (Callebaut Intense dark chocolate L-60-40NV or Ghirardelli bittersweet chocolate Baking Bar), melted and cooled. Cool chocolate to between 85 to 100 degrees before adding to frosting.
- 1/2 tsp vanilla extract

Direction

- Ganache Filling:
- Place chocolate, cream, and confectioners' sugar in medium microwave-safe bowl. Heat in microwave until mixture is warm to touch, 20-30 seconds. Whisk until smooth; transfer bowl to refrigerator and let stand until just chilled, no longer than 30 minutes.
- Cupcakes:
- Adjust oven rack to middle position and heat oven to 350 degrees. Line standard-size muffin pan (cups have 1/2 cup capacity) with baking-cup liners.
- Place chocolate and cocoa in medium bowl. Pour hot coffee over mixture and whisk until smooth. Set in refrigerator to cool completely, about 20 minutes.

- Whisk flour, sugar, salt, and baking soda together in medium bowl; set aside.
- Whisk oil, eggs, vinegar, and vanilla into cooled chocolate-cocoa mixture until smooth. Add flour mixture and whisk until smooth.
- Divide batter evenly among muffin pan cups. Place one slightly rounded teaspoon ganache filling on top of each cupcake.
- Bake until cupcakes are set and just firm to the touch, 17-19 minutes. Cool cupcakes in muffin pan on wire rack until cool enough to handle, about 10 minutes.
- Carefully lift each cupcake from muffin pan and set on wire rack. Cool to room temperature before frosting, about 1 hour. Frost and serve.
- Swiss Chocolate meringue buttercream Frosting:
- Combine sugar, egg whites, and salt in bowl of stand mixer; place bowl over pan of simmering water. Whisking gently but constantly, heat mixture until slightly thickened, foamy, and registers 150 degrees on instant-read thermometer, 2-3 minutes.
- Place bowl in stand mixer fitted with whisk attachment. Beat mixture on medium speed until consistency of shaving cream and slightly cooled, 1-2 minutes.
- Add butter, 1 piece at a time, until smooth and creamy. Once all butter is added, add cooled and melted chocolate and vanilla; mix until combined.
- Increase speed to medium-high and beat until light, fluffy, and thoroughly combined, about 30 seconds, scraping beater and sides of bowl with rubber spatula as necessary. Place finished frosting in microwave 5-10 seconds and stir 'til creamy if it becomes too thick to spread (if made in advance.)
- VARIATIONS:
- Creamy Malted Milk Chocolate Frosting:
- Follow recipe for Creamy Chocolate Frosting, reducing sugar to 1/4 cup, substituting milk chocolate for bittersweet chocolate, and adding 1/4 cup malted milk powder to frosting with vanilla extract in step 2.
- Creamy Vanilla Frosting:
- Follow recipe for Creamy Chocolate Frosting, omitting bittersweet chocolate and increasing sugar to 1/2 cup. (If final frosting seems too thick, warm mixer bowl briefly over pan of simmering water. Place bowl back on mixer and beat on medium-high until creamy.)
- Creamy Peanut Butter Frosting:
- Follow recipe for Creamy Chocolate Frosting, omitting bittersweet chocolate, increasing sugar to 1/2 cup and increasing salt to 1/8 tsp. Add 2/3 cup creamy peanut butter to frosting with vanilla extract in step 2. Garnish cupcakes with 1/2 cup chopped peanuts.
- Creamy Butterscotch Frosting:
- Follow recipe for Creamy Chocolate Frosting, substituting dark brown sugar for granulated sugar and increasing salt to 1/2 tsp.

174. Valentine Fairy Cakes Recipe

Serving: 18 | Prep: | Cook: 25mins | Ready in:

Ingredients

- 150 ml carton plain yogurt (rinse the pot and use as a measure)
- 1 pot of caster sugar
- 1 pot of sunflower oil
- 2 eggs
- 2 pots of self – raising flour
- 250 g strawberries plus extra for decorating, diced.
- Finely grated rind of 1 orange.
- For the icing and decoration
- 1 pot of icing sugar, plus extra for dusting
- 1 tbsp orange juice
- orange food coloring (optional)

Direction

- Preheat oven to 375 F. Line two muffins tray with 18 muffins paper cups.
- Beat the eggs and sugar until colour changes and batter is slightly thickened, add the oil in a

steady stream while beating, add the yogurt and mix well. Fold in the flour gently, add three quarters of the strawberries and half of the orange rind and fold again till combined. Don't overwork!! (I made it twice because of over beating)

- Fill each case three quarters full with the mixture and bake for 20-25 minutes until the cakes are risen and golden. Turn out and cool on a wire rack.
- Sift the icing sugar into a bowl; add the remaining orange rind and the orange juice to make a smooth icing. Stir in a few drops of orange food colouring, if you like.
- Using a teaspoon, spoon a little icing on top of each cooled cake .Decorate with extra strawberries or drizzled melted chocolate.

175. Valentines Day Red Velvet Cup Cakes Recipe

Serving: 18 | Prep: | Cook: 22mins |Ready in:

Ingredients

- 4 oz. NESTLÉ® TOLL HOUSE® CHOCOLATIER 62% Cacao
- bittersweet chocolate Baking Bar, broken into small pieces
- 1 1/4 cups all-purpose flour
- 1/2 teaspoon baking soda
- 1/2 teaspoon salt
- 3/4 cup milk
- 1 tablespoon white vinegar
- 1 cup granulated sugar
- 1/2 cup vegetable oil
- 3 large eggs
- 1 teaspoon vanilla extract
- 1 tablespoon red food coloring
- cream cheese frosting
- 1 pkg. (3 oz.) cream cheese, at room temperature
- 2 tablespoons butter, softened
- 2 tablespoons milk
- 1/2 teaspoon vanilla extract
- 3 cups powdered sugar
- Assorted sprinkles (optional)

Direction

- FOR CUPCAKES:
- PREHEAT oven to 350° F. Paper-line 18 muffin cups.
- MICROWAVE chocolate in small, uncovered, microwave-safe bowl on HIGH (100%) power for 45 seconds; STIR.
- If pieces retain some of their original shape, microwave at additional 10- to 15-second intervals, stirring just until melted.
- Cool to room temperature.
- COMBINE flour, baking soda and salt in small bowl.
- Combine milk and vinegar in small glass measure.
- Beat sugar, oil, eggs and vanilla extract in large mixer bowl on high for 2 minutes.
- Carefully beat in melted chocolate and red food colouring.
- Gradually beat in flour mixture alternately with milk mixture.
- Spoon into prepared muffin cups, filling 2/3 full.
- BAKE for 22 to 27 minutes or until wooden pick inserted in centres comes out clean.
- Cool in pan for 10 minutes; remove to wire racks to cool completely.
- Frost with Cream Cheese Frosting.
- Top with sprinkles, if desired.
- FOR CREAM CHEESE FROSTING:
- BEAT cream cheese, butter, milk and vanilla extract in medium mixer bowl until light and fluffy, scraping bowl occasionally.
- Gradually beat in powdered sugar until light and fluffy. Makes about 1 3/4 cups.
- TIPS:
- • You may substitute store bought cream cheese frosting (one 16-oz. container) to save time.
- • Frosting can be piped on with a pastry bag for a professional look.

176. Vanilla Bean Coconut Cupcakes With Coconut Frosting Recipe

Serving: 18 | Prep: | Cook: | Ready in:

Ingredients

- Reduced coconut milk:
- 2 13-to 14-ounce cans unsweetened coconut milk* (preferably organic)
- Cupcakes:
- 2 cups all purpose flour
- 2 1/4 teaspoons baking powder
- 1/2 teaspoon salt
- 3/4 cup (1 1/2 sticks) unsalted butter, room temperature
- 1 1/3 cups sugar
- 3 large eggs
- Seeds scraped from 1 split vanilla bean or 1 1/2 teaspoons vanilla extract
- 1 cup reduced coconut milk (see above), room temperature
- Frosting:
- 1 cup (2 sticks) unsalted butter, room temperature
- 2 1/2 cups powdered sugar
- 1/3 cup reduced coconut milk (see above), room temperature
- Seeds scraped from 1 split vanilla bean or 1 1/2 teaspoons vanilla extract
- 1/8 teaspoon salt
- 1 1/2 cups sweetened flaked coconut, lightly toasted (for garnish

Direction

- For reduced coconut milk:
- Bring coconut milk to boil in large deep saucepan over medium-high heat (coconut milk will boil up high in pan). Reduce heat to medium low; boil until reduced to 1 1/2 cups, stirring occasionally, 25 to 30 minutes. Remove from heat; cool completely. Transfer to small bowl. Cover; chill (coconut milk will settle slightly as it cools). DO AHEAD: Can be made 2 days ahead. Keep chilled.
- For cupcakes:
- Position rack in centre of oven; preheat to 350°F. Line eighteen 1/3-cup muffin cups with paper liners. Whisk flour, baking powder, and salt in medium bowl. Using electric mixer, beat butter in large bowl until smooth. Add sugar; beat on medium-high speed until well blended, about 2 minutes. Add 2 eggs, 1 at a time, beating well after each addition and occasionally scraping down sides of bowl. Beat in seeds from vanilla bean and remaining egg. Add half of flour mixture; mix on low speed just until blended. Add 1 cup reduced coconut milk; mix just until blended. Add remaining flour mixture; mix on low speed just until blended. Divide batter among muffin cups. Bake cupcakes until tops spring back when gently touched and tester inserted into centre comes out clean, about 20 minutes. Transfer cupcakes in pans to rack; cool 10 minutes. Carefully remove cupcakes from pans and cool completely on rack.
- For frosting:
- Using electric mixer, beat butter in large bowl until smooth. Add sugar, 1/3 cup reduced coconut milk, seeds from vanilla bean, and salt. Beat on medium-low speed until blended, scraping down sides of bowl. Increase to medium high and beat until light and fluffy.
- Using pastry bag fitted with large star tip, pipe frosting onto cooled cupcakes. (Alternatively, top each cupcake with 2 tablespoons frosting. Using small offset spatula, swirl frosting over top of cupcakes, leaving 1/2-inch plain border.) Sprinkle with coconut. DO AHEAD: Can be made 1 day ahead. Store in airtight containers; chill. Bring to room temperature before serving.
- * Available at many supermarkets and at Indian, Southeast Asian, and Latin markets.

177. Vanilla Cupcake With Fruit Topping Recipe

Serving: 12 | Prep: | Cook: 20mins | Ready in:

Ingredients

- 1 1/2 cups all purpose flour
- 1/4 teaspoon salt
- 1 1/2 teaspoons baking powder
- 1/2 cup butter, unsalted, room temperature
- 2/3 cup sugar
- 3 eggs, room temperature
- 1/4 cup milk
- 1 teaspoon pure vanilla extract
- Zest of 1 large lemon (optional)
- Sliced fruits
- light whipped topping

Direction

- Preheat oven to 375f degree; line muffin cups with paper liners.
- In a large bowl, beaten butter and sugar till light and fluffy using electric mixer. Add eggs, one at a time, beating well after each addition. Beat in the vanilla extract and lemon zest.
- In a separate medium bowl, whisk together the flour, baking powder, and salt.
- With the mixer on low speed, alternately add the flour mixture and milk, in three additions, beginning and ending with the flour. Scrape down the sides of the bowl.
- Divide evenly among pans and bake for 20 minutes or until nicely browned and a toothpick inserted into a cupcake comes out clean
- Remove from oven and place on a wire rack to cool.
- Once the cupcakes have completely cooled, using a small knife, cut a shallow dip in the top of each cupcake.
- Top with fruit and whipped topping.

178. Warm Chocolate Cupcake With Decadent Soft Chocolate Center Recipe

Serving: 6 | Prep: | Cook: 12mins | Ready in:

Ingredients

- For cupcakes:
- 2 tablespoons melted butter for brushing cups
- 5 ounces bittersweet or semisweet chocolate (best quality chocolate only please, such as Scharffen Berger or Valrhona)
- 10 tablespoons butter
- 3 large organic eggs
- 3 large organic egg yolks
- 1/4 cup sugar
- 3 tablespoons all-purpose flour
- For chocolate Raspberry Truffles:
- 4 ounces best quality bittersweet or semisweet chocolate, cut into small pieces
- 3 tablespoons heavy cream
- 1 tablespoon (1/2 ounce) unsalted butter
- 2 tablespoons flavoring of your choice, such as Grand Marnier, Amaretto, raspberry liqueur, etc.
- best quality cocoa powder for coating

Direction

- For cupcakes:
- Thoroughly brush the insides of 6 8-ounce custard cups, ramekins or jumbo muffin tin with melted butter. Pre-heat oven to 350 degrees F.
- In the top of a double boiler or medium heatproof bowl set over simmering water, melt chocolate and butter. Remove from heat.
- In large bowl of electric mixer beat eggs, egg yolks and sugar for about 5 minutes or until they are pale yellow, thick and creamy.
- Fold egg mixture into chocolate mixture about one third at a time. Gently fold in flour. Pour mixture into prepared cups filling about two thirds full. If using Chocolate Raspberry Truffles, fill the cups halfway then pop a truffle into the centre of the batter of each one,

- spooning the last of the batter over the truffles to enclose them completely before baking.
- Bake for 10 to 12 minutes. (The sides of the cakes should be firm but the centres will still be soft.) Remove from oven and set aside to cool for about 10 minutes before unmoulding.
- Serve with sweetened whipped cream, shaved chocolate and fresh raspberries.
- If you want a taste that will perfectly reflect the richness of the chocolate in this dessert think about serving a small glass of Godiva Chocolate liqueur. If you seek a contrast turn to Champagne, and pile decadence on top of decadence!
- For Raspberry truffles:
- In a small heatproof bowl set over but not touching simmering water, combine the chocolate, cream, and butter. When the chocolate has almost melted, remove the bowl from the heat and stir the mixture until smooth. Stir in the flavouring of your choice, cover the bowl, and refrigerate, stirring occasionally, until the mixture is thick enough to mound on a spoon, about 30 minutes.
- 2. Line a baking try with waxed or parchment paper. Scrape the chocolate mixture into a pastry bag fitted with a #3 plain tip. Pipe eight 1-inch mounds onto the prepared tray. Put the baking tray in the refrigerator and chill the truffles until firm, about 15 minutes.
- 3. Spread some cocoa powder on a plate or in a bowl. Gently roll each truffle between your hands to give it a ball shape, and then lightly roll it in the powder to coat it. Transfer to a plate and store in a cool place until serving.

179. White Chocolate Macadamia Nut Cupcakes Recipe

Serving: 20 | Prep: | Cook: 20mins | Ready in:

Ingredients

- 1 package white cake mix without pudding in the mix
- Ingredients needed for cake mix
- 1 package (4 servings) white chocolate instant pudding and pie filling mix
- 3/4 cup chopped macadamia nuts
- 1 1/2 cups flaked coconut
- 1 cup white chocolate chips
- 1 (16 oz) can white frosting

Direction

- Preheat oven to 350 degrees
- Line muffin tin with 20 baking cups
- Prepare cake mix according to box, mixing in pudding mix
- Fold in Nuts
- Spoon into muffin cups, filling 2/3 full
- Bake 18-20 minutes
- Cool cupcakes on wire rack
- Spread coconut on baking sheet and toast at 350 degrees for about 6 minutes until golden brown. Cool slightly.
- Microwave chocolate chips until melted, usually takes about 2 minutes stirring every 30 seconds
- Mix melted white chocolate chips into frosting
- Frost cupcakes and top with toasted coconut

180. White Chocolate Mousse In Milk Chocolate Shells Recipe

Serving: 8 | Prep: | Cook: 240mins | Ready in:

Ingredients

- Mousse
- 4 1/2 oz. white chocolate baking bar, cut up
- 1 1/2 cups whipping cream
- 3/4 teaspoon vanilla
- Shells
- 1 (7-oz.) bar milk chocolate, cut up
- 1 tablespoon oil

Direction

- DIRECTIONS
- 1. In small saucepan, combine white chocolate baking bar and whipping cream; heat over low heat, stirring constantly until baking bar is melted and smooth.
- 2. Stir in vanilla. Pour into small bowl; cover with plastic wrap. Refrigerate 4 hours or overnight until mixture is very cold and thickened, stirring occasionally.
- 3. Line 8 muffin cups with foil or paper baking cups. In small saucepan, combine milk chocolate and oil; heat over low heat, stirring until chocolate is melted and smooth. Remove from heat.
- 4. With small paint brush, pastry brush or teaspoon, brush thin layer of chocolate evenly over sides and bottom of each foil cup. Place in freezer until firm, about 5 minutes. Repeat coating process of cups using remaining chocolate. Place in freezer until firm, 10 to 20 minutes.
- 5. Carefully peel foil cups from chocolate shells; place shells in refrigerator while preparing filling. With electric mixer, beat white chocolate mixture at high speed until light and fluffy. DO NOT OVERBEAT.
- 6. To serve, spoon 1/2 cup mousse into each chocolate shell. If desired, garnish with stemmed maraschino cherry. Store in refrigerator.

181. White Russian Cupcakes Recipe

Serving: 2024 | Prep: | Cook: 18mins | Ready in:

Ingredients

- 18 1/4 ounces yellow cake mix
- 3 1/2 ounces vanilla instant pudding mix
- 1 cup vegetable oil
- 3/4 cup whole milk
- 4 large eggs
- 1/4 cup vodka
- 1/4 cup Kahlua, plus
- 2 teaspoons Kahlua, divided
- 1 teaspoon pure vanilla extract
- frosting
- 1 cup heavy cream
- 2 tablespoons powdered sugar
- 1 tablespoon Kahlua
- 2 tablespoons semisweet chocolate, shavings

Direction

- Cupcakes:
- Preheat oven to 350°F and line 24 cupcake cups with paper liners.
- Place cake mix, pudding mix, oil, milk, eggs, vodka, 1/4 cup Kahlua, and vanilla in a large mixing bowl.
- Blend with an electric mixer on low speed for 30 seconds. Stop the machine and scrape down the sides of the bowl. Increase the mixer speed to medium and beat 2 minutes more, scraping down the sides again if needed.
- Spoon or scoop 1/3 cup batter into each lined cupcake cup, filling it three quarters of the way full. (Remove empty liners if you don't get the full 24 cupcakes).
- Bake until they are golden and spring back when lightly pressed with your finger, about 17-20 minutes. Remove the pans from the oven and place them on wire racks.
- Cool for 5 minutes. Brush the tops of the cupcakes with remaining 2 tablespoons Kahlua.
- Remove cupcakes from pans. Place on wire rack to cool.
- Frosting:
- Place a large, clean mixing bowl and electric mixer beaters into the freezer to chill for 1 minute. Remove the bowl and beaters from the freezer.
- Pour the heavy cream into the bowl and beat with electric mixer on high speed until the cream has thickened, 1 1/2 minutes.
- Stop the machine and add the sugar and 1 tablespoon Kahlua.
- Beat the cream on high speed until stiff peaks form, 1-2 more minutes.

- Place a heaping tablespoon of the whipped cream on each cupcake and swirl to spread it out with a short metal spatula or spoon, taking care to cover tops completely.
- Garnish with chocolate shavings.

182. Whole Wheat Cupcakes Recipe

Serving: 24 | Prep: | Cook: 20mins | Ready in:

Ingredients

- 1/2 cup butter
- 2/3 cup brown sugar
- 1/2 cup honey
- 1 teaspoon vanilla extract
- 2 large eggs
- 2 cups stone ground whole wheat flour
- 1/2 tablespoon baking powder
- 1/2 teaspoon baking soda
- 1 teaspoon salt
- 1/2 teaspoon cinnamon
- 1/4 teaspoon nutmeg
- 1 cup grated unpeeled apples
- 2/3 cup chopped walnuts
- For the frosting (may be optional)
- 4 ounces cream cheese
- 1/4 cup butter
- 2 cups powdered sugar
- 1 tablespoon water

Direction

- Preheat the oven to 375 degrees.
- Line a regular muffin tin with paper liners.
- Cream the butter and brown sugar together.
- Add the honey, eggs, and vanilla extract and beat together.
- Whisk the flour, baking powder, baking soda, salt, cinnamon, and nutmeg together in another bowl.
- Add about one-third of the flour mixture to the creamed mixture, then about one-half of the apples.
- Repeat with the flour, then apples, then flour to complete the mixing.
- Mix until just combined.
- Add the nuts.
- Spoon the batter into the muffin cups.
- The recipe will make about 24 cupcakes.
- Bake 18 to 20 minutes or until done.
- Let it cool on a wire rack.
- For the frosting, mix the cream cheese and butter together.
- Add the powdered sugar and the water a bit at time and mix to a spreadable consistency.

183. Wigglin Jigglin Halloween Cupcakes Recipe

Serving: 24 | Prep: | Cook: 30mins | Ready in:

Ingredients

- 2 1/2 cups boiling water (Do not add cold water.)
- 2 (6-ounce each) packages Jell-O Brand orange flavor gelatin
- 1 (18.25-ounce) package yellow cake mix
- 1 (8-ounce) tub Cool Whip whipped topping, thawed
- Halloween sprinkles

Direction

- Stir boiling water into dry gelatine mix in medium bowl at least 3 minutes until completely dissolved. Pour into 15 x 10 x 1-inch pan. Refrigerate at least 3 hours or until firm.
- Meanwhile, prepare and bake cake mix as directed on package for 24 cupcakes. Cool completely on wire racks. Cut each cupcake in half horizontally.
- Dip bottom of 15 x 10 x 1-inch pan in warm water about 15 seconds.

- Using 2-inch round cookie cutter, cut out 24 Jigglers®.
- Place a small dollop of whipped topping on bottom half of each cupcake; top with Jigglers® circle and another small dollop of whipped topping.
- Place top half of cupcake on each stack and gently press into whipped topping.
- Top with remaining whipped topping and sprinkles.

184. White Chocolate Macadamia Cupcakes Recipe

Serving: 20 | Prep: | Cook: 20mins | Ready in:

Ingredients

- 1 package white cake mix, plus ingredients to prepare cake.
- 1 package hite chocolate instant pudding and pie mix
- 3/4 cup chopped macadamia nuts
- 1 1/2 cups flaked coconut
- ` cup white chocolate chips
- 1 container white frosting

Direction

- Preheat oven to 350 degrees. Line muffin tins with paper liners.
- Prepare cake mix according to directions, beating in pudding mix with cake mix ingredients. Fold in nuts.
- Fill muffin cups 2/3 full.
- Bake 18-20 minutes, or until a toothpick comes out clean.
- Cool in pans on wire racks 10 minutes. Remove from pans and cool completely.
- Meanwhile, spread coconut evenly on ungreased baking sheet. Bake 350 degrees 6 minutes, stirring occasionally, until light brown. Cool completely.
- Place white chocolate chips in microwave bowl; microwave 2 minutes on medium setting, stirring every 30 seconds, until melted and smooth. Cool slightly before stirring into frosting.
- Frost cupcakes, and top with toasted coconut.

185. Yellow Cake Cupcakes Recipe

Serving: 12 | Prep: | Cook: 25mins | Ready in:

Ingredients

- 1 1/2 cups unbleached all-purpose flour
- 1/2 teaspoon table salt
- 1/2 cup sour cream
- 1 cup granulated sugar (7 ounces)
- 1 1/2 teaspoons baking powder
- 1 large egg , room temperature
- 1 stick unsalted butter, room temperature
- 2 large egg yolks , room temperature
- 1 1/2 teaspoons vanilla extract

Direction

- Preheat your oven to 350F and make sure you have a middle rack. Line your cupcake tin with paper or foil liners.
- Whisk sugar, flour, salt and baking powder in the bowl of a standing mixer fitted with paddle attachment.
- Add butter, egg, sour cream, egg yolks, and vanilla. Beat this at medium speed until smooth, (approx. 30 seconds).
- Pour your batter in your cupcake tin evenly and then bake until light golden brown. The cupcakes are ready when a toothpick poke in the centre of the cupcake comes out clean.
- Let these cool for about 45 minutes.

Index

A
Ale 12
Apple 3,6,16,23

B
Bacon 3,8
Baking 102,104
Banana 3,10,11,12,16
Beer 5,90
Berry 4,74
Biscuits 4,75
Bran 109
Butter 3,4,5,20,21,28,30,31,33,34,36,39,42,43,46,47,48,66,68,76,79,91,99,102,103

C
Cake 3,4,5,15,17,18,24,41,47,50,55,57,60,62,69,79,80,87,90,100,103,104,110
Caramel 3,23
Carrot 3,4,24,25,27,35,69,81
Champ 107
Cheese 3,4,5,12,14,15,24,25,26,30,40,42,43,53,67,69,84,85,88,95,98,104
Chocolate 3,4,5,12,18,19,20,22,28,29,30,31,32,33,34,35,36,38,40,42,43,44,46,50,52,53,54,56,61,75,80,83,89,99,101,102,103,106,107,110
Cinnamon 3,6,14,38,39

Coconut 3,4,5,22,40,62,81,105
Cranberry 4,80
Cream 3,4,5,8,9,11,12,13,14,15,17,19,24,25,26,30,35,40,41,42,43,44,45,53,67,69,75,76,84,85,88,89,91,95,98,102,103,104,109
Curd 68

E
Egg 4,30,49,52

F
Fat 3,4,8,30,49,93
Flour 46
Fruit 5,106

G
Gin 3,5,25,85

H
Heart 5,99
Honey 4,61

I
Icing 3,4,30,31,40,43,52,53,55,61

J
Jelly 4,79
Jus 7,22,98

L
Lemon 4,38,65,66,67,68,70,75,78
Lime 4,5,45,64,96

M
Macadamia 5,107,110
Mace 93
Mandarin 4,71
Marshmallow 3,4,6,48
Meat 8

Meringue 3,4,33,45,67,68

Milk 4,5,54,80,99,103,107

Mint 3,33

Muffins 3,4,5,6,10,11,16,23,25,29,32,34,36,49,53,77,78,80,89,99,101

N

Nut 3,4,5,13,29,56,76,77,86,98,107

O

Oatmeal 4,77

Orange 4,38,49,61,71

P

Peach 4,78

Peanut butter 32

Pecan 4,80

Peel 80

Pepper 4,5,82,84

Pie 3,17

Pineapple 4,81

Pistachio 5,83

Plum 5,83

Port 89

Pulse 39,55,69

Pumpkin 3,4,5,21,51,80,84,85

R

Raspberry 3,4,27,46,68,106,107

Rice 4,78

Ricotta 3,4,34,75

Royal icing 75

S

Seeds 105

Soda 92

Sponge cake 100

Strawberry 3,5,30,31,93,95,96,97,98,99

Sugar 4,10,47,93

T

Tea 92

Truffle 79,106

W

Walnut 5,83

Z

Zest 67,106

Conclusion

Thank you again for downloading this book!

I hope you enjoyed reading about my book!

If you enjoyed this book, please take the time to share your thoughts and post a review on Amazon. It'd be greatly appreciated!

Write me an honest review about the book – I truly value your opinion and thoughts and I will incorporate them into my next book, which is already underway.

Thank you!

If you have any questions, **feel free to contact at:** author@bisquerecipes.com

Angela Haas

bisquerecipes.com

Printed in Great Britain
by Amazon